To **Kerry**, my amazing wife and partner for all the
support over the years. My rock and soulmate! 10 sky.
And my little rocks too, **Oliver**, **Esmé** and **Vincent**.
And, of course, my Jack Russell, **Whoops**, for listening.

Cracking
Yolks
& Pig
Tales

The lid off life in the kitchen
with 110 stunning recipes

Glynn Purnell

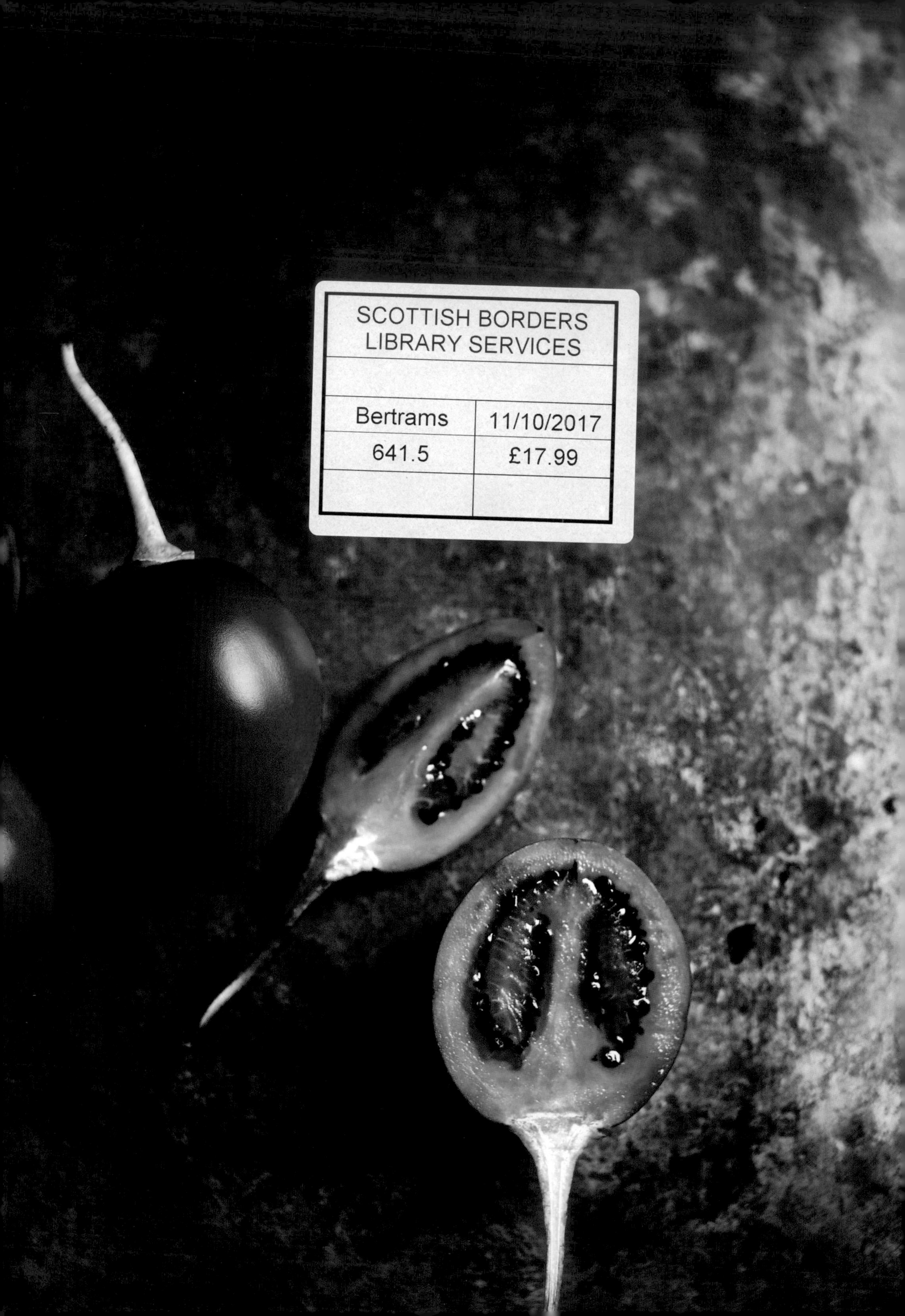

Contents

Introduction   6

1   Eggs, soups & sausages   10

2   What's next - hot, cold or frozen?   40

3   Fins, shells & tentacles   66

4   Hoof, horn, snout & tail   94

5   Shy babies get no sweets   124

6   Stocks, pots & bread rolls   168

Index   204

Acknowledgements   207

It all started for me as a child.

I was brought up on a council estate in Birmingham in a loving family. My dad was a hard-working factory man, my mum was a cleaner and a dinner lady. I have two sisters, Gaynor and Gemma, plus a little brother, Gareth, also known as Gazzyboy. Food was really important at home. Everything was homemade and my mum was a great cook. We'd have lots of fresh veg and offal, never a frozen chip in sight! Mum would cook during the week, but my dad, who loved watching Keith Floyd, Ken Hom and Madhur Jaffery on the TV, was let loose at the weekend. This meant that one weekend would be Indian, the next my dad would get the wok out, and so on. It really inspired me to cook and try new flavours. On Saturdays, I'd go on trips to the Bull Ring market with my mum to bring back the meat and fish, plus (sometimes) a special treat, such as a little tub of cockles with white pepper and vinegar, a big nasty whelk or some pig's trotters! The pig's trotters would be boiled up and then eaten with a packet of crisps in my pyjamas while watching Blind Date, which meant I would be going to bed with sticky PJs.

When Mum was working, Dad was doing overtime and Gaynor was at her Saturday job at the hairdressers, I would look after Gazzyboy and Gemma. I loved to try out dishes on them. The first was beans on toast. I'd get a bit of onion and a teaspoon of curry powder in with the baked beans, put the beans on the toast and cover it with cheese. Or I would put grated cheese in the bottom of a bowl of soup, which was always a winner. #stringycheese. I thought I was a genius – and so did my brother and sister.

On special occasions, we would be taken to a curry house for a balti, in a little place called The Falcon. It wasn't licensed, so Mum would always bring a bottle of tiger milk and my dad would take four cans of lager. We would order our baltis and a naan bread, which we called table naan, aka bread duvet. It was always epic! The balti dishes would come out sizzling and my dad would always say, 'Don't touch. They're hot!' But I couldn't help myself. I think every true Brummie has a balti burn . . .

Being brought up in a large family surrounded by food and challenged with spices and things like pig's trotters, set me well and truly on my way. I learnt to respect produce, the cost of it and the importance of food. When I was 14, I began washing up and making salads for a hotel lounge. I loved it. I was kept in line by a big German lady called Lisa. You didn't mess with her! She looked after me like a son and would make me drink a pint of carrot juice a day and eat massive German sausages, as she always said I was too thin.

I was hungry for more knowledge, though, so when I left school I pushed for apprenticeships. A lovely woman called Tina Morris who was in HR at the hotel really helped make it happen. I worked in the main kitchen under Peter Wintle and a larger-than-life character called Roger Kendrick. What a legend. R.I.P x. Roger was Peter's right-hand man; he made me cry, laugh, love and hate the job. After a while banging out big

banquets and dinners it was time to move on to the hotel restaurant, The Terrace, but when I got there I shit myself. It was the elite kitchen, the A-Team, and I was the whipping boy. The head chef who ran it was Tony Morrin. He was perceived as a bit of a nutter, but it was his passion for food, a perfection that made him a great chef. Tony helped me so much with everything, sending me first to Gary Rhodes for a stage, then to Aubergine, which was run by an amazing up-and-coming chef called Gordon Ramsay.

The sous-chef at The Terrace, Mark Hill, was the one who cooked the meat and fish. I was his commis (apprentice) and when I first started he would call me 'Oi'. Mark was a right grumpy fucker but I learnt a lot from him and grew to love him. We would wash up all our own pans, he would never let anyone else touch them because, as he said, 'They're ours!' I always knew I was going to be a meat chef after my time at The Terrace. I did a little stint on the larder with Sharon Cooney, a fantastic larder chef, but even she missed the heat and aggression of the stoves.

After years of being pushed, slapped and kicked, I moved onto the next part of my apprenticeship, the pastry. But I thought that was for girls, so I went in kind of sulking. Back then, the hotel would bake and make everything apart from banqueting bread, which was pretty impressive. I soon learned to love pastry. It took me a couple of weeks to get how it works, but I really loved it. I worked for a very clever and organised guy called Vic Jones, who knew everything from how to make 2,000 cheesecakes to a wonderful sweet trolley; only one problem – he was a Villa fan. So I finished my apprenticeship having done burgers, washing up, prepping racks of lamb, room service, waiting and accounts. Looking back, I had a brilliant schooling, both in cooking and in life.

From The Terrace, I went to work at Simpson's in Kenilworth for seven years, under the chef patron Andreas Antona. There was a real family feeling about the place, with Alison, Andreas's wife, in the front of house. I learned a huge amount, not just cooking, but about the restaurant industry as a whole. The two main chefs, Luke Tipping and Andy Waters, taught me loads, but it was Andreas who really looked after me. He put money in my pocket when I was skint and sent me on stages in France and even paid for the flights. He really pushed me forward. It was invaluable knowledge that helped us gain a Michelin star – an achievement I was made to celebrate by having the Michelin man tattooed on my leg, but that's another story.

> It was invaluable knowledge that helped us gain a Michelin star – an achievement I was made to celebrate by having the Michelin man tattooed on my leg, but that's another story!

I was then incredibly fortunate to work for another chef patron, Claude Bosi, who taught me to be myself and develop my own style. In my opinion, he is the most naturally talented chef I've seen cook and one of the best in the country. At Hibiscus, in what back then was a little Shropshire market town called Ludlow, I would work 18 hours a day, 6 days a week. I could write a book on what happened during the short time I was there, from staff running away in the night, so me, Claude and a Japanese stagier called 'Yousy' get it right in the arse, to the dogs Didier and Flea in the kitchen and countless Michelin inspections. The cooking was wild. All the meat was cooked on the bone, as was all the fish, plus there were snails, frogs, whole pigs and foraging every week. I loved the produce we got. Claude had one Michelin star when I started and I was delighted when, in the next guide, he had two. Claude is a master chef and was well on the way to two stars with or without me, but I am very proud to have been a part of the team when he gained his second. And watch this space, as I'm sure his third will come to him in London.

After Hibiscus, I was ready to become the chef and cook my own food. Keith and Diane

Stevenson, big foodies from Sutton Coldfield, wanted to open their own place, with me heading up the kitchen. It was a life-changing opportunity. We opened Jessica's on a small budget, just outside the red-light district in Birmingham. There were only two of us in the kitchen – me and my sous chef, 'Sandwich' – and out front we had Pascal, the restaurant manager, and Renault, his assistant. It was brutal; we worked 6 days a week, 18 hours a day, drank a bottle of wine a night, and slept in the laundry for half an hour on our break. The hard work paid off, though. We smashed it, winning Birmingham's first Michelin star and AA Restaurant of the Year. We got great reviews from some of Britain's biggest food critics and I had 20 per cent of the business. I was almost living the dream. Something, though, was missing. I had always wanted to be the boss and to have my own restaurant. I woke up one day and said to my partner Kerry, 'We are going alone.' We had just got our first little house and our first child, Oliver, was two years old. Her face dropped because it was the first time in our lives together we were living comfortably. I had been at Jessica's for just over four years and, when I left, Jessica's folded at the same time. I took twenty grand out of my house, raided my piggy bank, smashed my credit cards and went to the bank. The bank gave me a lot of no's and I was faced with lots of slamming doors but my accountant and good friend Mike Vousden spoke with the bank manager, Paul Reid, and made it happen. I took out a loan with a company that deals in grants called 'Art', who were great, and with the bank on side, Mike and I wrote my business plan and we were off. I found a site in town, 55 Cornwall Street, an old Victorian warehouse being used as a furniture shop. I had a really low budget, so had to be a little bit clever with my money. I paid the furniture guy and builders half of the bill upfront and promised to pay the remainder a month after opening, which turned out to be a rough first four weeks. We made just enough for the builders, furniture guy, staff and bills, leaving me with only enough to buy a bag of sweets. It's been a great journey since, though, and it feels as if it's just the start. Purnell's Restaurant opened in 2007 on the seventh day of the seventh month at 7pm. Lucky number 7, eh? Now, almost seven years on, the restaurant has gone from strength to strength and I have been involved in TV programmes such as *Great British Menu*, *Saturday Kitchen*, and *Great British Food Revival* and I believe there is still loads to come for me and the restaurant. We are still striving and pushing forward and we now have Purnell's Bistro and Ginger's Bar, both of which are flourishing.

> It was brutal; we worked 6 days a week, 18 hours a day, drank a bottle of wine a night, and slept in the laundry for half an hour on our break.

My family has grown, too, and we now have three little people. Ginge, Oliver, our eldest, Esme Summer, the princess, and our youngest, Vincent, aka Bam Bam. As for my restaurant family, I've had some great staff over the years, including my long-serving manager, Jean-Benoit Burloux (now sadly left). My new manager, Sonal Clare, my two sous chefs, Dave Taylor and Luke Butcher, and my PA, who is also my sister-in-law, Angela O'Carroll. Pete Casson, my pastry chef, who now runs my bistro and, of course, my soulmate, lover and mother of my children, Kerry. It's certainly been an adventure!

This is not a restaurant cookbook or a home cookbook; it's just a cookbook. If you want to cook a challenging dish from the restaurant such as haddock, eggs and cornflakes, you'll find it here. If you want to cook something a bit more down to earth, such as faggots and peas, it's also here. If you want to flick through it and then use it to prop up a wonky table, it's good for that too. Enjoy the book, there's some swearing, some true stories (which may have been slightly exaggerated because my memory isn't that great) and loads of great recipes. Try them. They all work, promise.

Eggs
Soups
& Sausages

The pillow fight

This happened years ago, when I was much more rock n' roll – I don't tend to go around smashing up hotels! Daniel Clifford, a two Michelin star chef from Cambridge and a great friend of mine, was supposed to come with us. At 2am, when we were slightly pissed, we rang him leaving him message after message, about 25–30, which really pissed him off, but he later saw the funny side.

It all started on a road trip up North with Claude Bosi, my old head chef from Hibiscus, Shane Osborn, who at the time was head chef at Pied à Terre, Tom Kerridge, of the Hand and Flowers, and, of course, the man, Sat Bains. It began with a fantastic dinner. We were loud. Like so loud other diners were moved away from us. I remember one couple trying to enjoy an anniversary meal and to help them celebrate we sent over a bottle of Champagne. We also sent drinks to other diners, so it ended up costing a fucking fortune.

As I said, we were creating a bit of noise. Not in a bad way, we were just enthusiastic. As the night wore on we carried on drinking and started to get into morning territory. Claude, with his trousers rolled up, began throwing empty bottles of Champagne as he chased ducks around the stream (he has never been good at pulling the birds). I stripped to my pants and decided to throw some furniture around. As I tired of this game, I sat in the middle of the stream sipping on Champagne, laughing my head off.

We stayed over in a lovely cottage, which was proper beautiful. Well it was, until we'd lived there for a night. Everyone started to go to bed. The Frenchman and I were sharing. Tom had his own room and Sat bunked up with Shane the Ozzie. We were all getting changed when Claude said, 'Let's go and take out Sat and Shane.' I thought, fucking great idea! So, dressed only in our boxer shorts and pillows in hand, we crept around the corner and smashed open the door. Only to be confronted by Sat, sitting ready at the end of the bed. To this day, I am not 100 per cent sure, but I think he was wearing silk pyjama bottoms.

As we all know, Sat is massive. I mean a mass of muscle! Claude shouted; 'Fucking 'ave it,' and I just threw myself, waist high, at the big man. Sat hurled his pillow at me, with him still attached, and completely smashed me across the room. I fell on top of a coffee table, which had a massive porcelain lamp on it, and it exploded into bits on impact. Surrounded by broken lamp, I looked up to see Claude standing by the door, laughing his bollocks off. As were Sat and Shane. Then, before I knew it, it proper went off! Four big, half-naked chefs were rolling around with pillows, smashing and banging, with the odd touch of silk pyjamas thrown into the mix. After it calmed down, we all looked at each other, sweating and laughing and, for that split second, thought . . . gay!

We got up and tried to sort out the room, still really pissed. The funniest thing was that Sat took ages gathering the broken lamp. He swept the pieces into a big pile and strategically placed the lamp on top, saying; 'They will never know . . .'

You may be wondering where Tom was in all of this. In the background, all we could hear was someone dragging concrete - well that's what it sounded like. It was actually Tom snoring. Unbeknown to us, he'd fucked off to bed!

It was one of the wildest, funniest... #roadtrip dinners I have ever been on. I will always remember being woken up by the sound of Tom's alarm. The fucking noise went on for about an hour, accompanied by the slow sound of dragging concrete and him not even stirring. (No pun intended.)

Anyway, the moral of the story is: never rely on a Frenchman when going into battle and always make sure you don't ever pick a fight with a man wearing silk pyjamas who is twice your size!

Watercress and Wasabi Pea Soup

Peppery, smooth and with a little heat. What me? Ha ha! No, although a great description. These ingredients - fresh green watercress and spinach, fiery wasabi peas and juicy water chestnuts - make a great team. Watercress is one of my favourite ingredients; a little retro, but it's making a great comeback. It's the George Foreman of lettuce and wow what a soup it makes.

1. Heat a saucepan with a little vegetable oil and sweat the onion and garlic over a gentle heat until soft.

2. Add the potatoes, cover with half the stock and simmer for 20 minutes, or until the potatoes are tender.

3. Add the spinach and watercress and simmer until wilted, then add the remainder of the stock, the nutmeg and the ginger.

4. Simmer for a further 5 minutes, then whizz in a blender until smooth and pass through a sieve.

1. Using a pestle and mortar, crush the peas and peppercorns, then add to the soured cream in a bowl and mix together.

2. Place the soured cream mixture in serving bowls and evenly sprinkle with the water chestnut slices. Pour the soup over the top. Serve with bread.

Serves 4

For the soup
splash of vegetable oil
1 onion, peeled and diced
1 garlic clove, peeled and smashed
100g potatoes, peeled and chopped
1 litre chicken or vegetable stock
400g picked spinach
400g picked watercress
grating of nutmeg
pinch of ground ginger

To garnish
2 tablespoons wasabi peas
10 black peppercorns
150g soured cream
150g drained canned water
  chestnuts, thinly sliced
simple white loaf, to serve (see
  page 172)

Butternut Squash Soup with Orange, Szechuan Pepper and Truffled Feta Terrine

Butternut squash always reminds me of autumn – the colour in particular. This is a simple soup without all the garnish bit. I love how the Szechuan pepper and the orange bring out the saltiness of the feta. The marriage between the orange and the squash also takes me back to my mentor and friend, Claude Bosi. He would combine the squash with sharp passion fruit – genius!

1. Heat a large saucepan with a little butter or vegetable oil and sweat the onion and carrots over a gentle heat until softened.

2. Add the garlic and squash and cook for about 10 minutes until the squash begins to soften.

3. Add half the stock with a light seasoning of salt and black pepper and simmer briskly for 5 minutes.

4. Add the remainder of the stock and simmer for about 10 minutes until the vegetables are tender.

5. Whizz the soup in a blender until smooth and season to taste with salt and black pepper.

1. Put the milk and feta with the chopped truffle and truffle oil in a saucepan and bring to the boil.

2. Add the agar agar and cook, stirring, for 1 minute.

3. Pour the mixture into a 17 x 22cm baking tray, at least 3cm deep, and leave in the fridge for about 2 hours until set.

1. Mix the ingredients for the oil together in a saucepan and cook over a low heat for at least 1 hour for maximum flavour.

2. Remove from the heat and strain through a sieve.

Cut the terrine into 2cm-square pieces and place four or five cubes in each bowl. Drizzle with the orange oil and add a twist of black pepper. Decant the soup into a large jug and serve over the terrine at the table.

Serves 4

For the butternut squash
knob of butter or splash of
  vegetable oil
1 onion, peeled and chopped
3 carrots, peeled and chopped
2 garlic cloves, peeled
2 medium butternut squash,
  peeled, deseeded and chopped
2 litres chicken stock
salt and ground ginger

For the feta terrine
100g full-fat milk
200g feta, crumbled
16g truffle, chopped
2g truffle oil
2g agar agar

For the orange oil
zest of 5 oranges
1 heaped teaspoon ground
  Szechuan pepper
400ml sunflower oil
freshly ground black pepper

'Birmingham Soup' 1793

This dish makes me smile because people have always taken the piss out of Brum, saying it has no food culture other than curry. Bullshit! It's a reinvention of a soup made by Matthew Boulton, who was one of the captains of industry in the late 1700s. He sold to his workers for an old penny; it's costs a bit more now in my restaurant.

Although it involves several steps, it's well worth the effort. At the restaurant, we serve it with smoked bone marrow, foie gras butter (see page 185) and, best of all, pikelets (page 178), not crumpets - unless you want a fight, that is.

---

1. Preheat the oven to 200°C/gas mark 6.

2. Heat a frying pan until medium hot, add the ox cheek and render the fat until the cheek is golden brown. Remove from the pan and place in a deep roasting tin.

3. Deglaze the frying pan with the red wine, scraping up the sediment from the base of the pan.

4. Place all the vegetables on top of the cheek along with the herb sprigs and pour the wine over the top. Completely cover with the boiling water.

5. Cover the roasting tin tightly with foil and braise the ox cheek in the oven for 4 hours.

6. Remove from the oven and leave to cool in the liquor for about 1 hour.

7. Lift the ox cheek out and remove and discard any fat and sinew. Place on a flat tray and keep warm until ready to serve, covering if necessary.

1. Preheat the oven to 200°C/gas mark 6.

2. Soak the pieces of bone in cold water for 1 hour until the marrow can be easily pushed out.

Using a smoker
1. Place the hay and smoking chips in the bottom of a smoker and burn until smoking, following the manufacturer's instructions.

2. Place the bone marrow on the perforated smoking tray and leave to smoke for 4 minutes

Alternative method
1. Place the hay and smoking chips into a frying pan and set alight with a match.

2. Leave to burn until smouldering and then tip the smouldering ash into a glass bowl

3. Place a metal colander on top of the bowl and place the bone marrow in the colander.

4. Wrap the entire bowl and colander in cling film and leave to smoke for 6 minutes.

After smoking
5. Dice the bone marrow into 1cm cubes, place on roasting tray and warm through in the oven for about 3 minutes until just beginning to melt.

6. Place the bone marrow pieces on top of the braised cheeks ready to serve.

SERVES 4

For the braised ox cheek
1 ox cheek, untrimmed/fat on
¼ bottle (190ml) of red wine
1 carrot, peeled and cut into
  2.5cm pieces
2 celery sticks, cut into 2.5cm pieces
1 onion, peeled and cut into
  2.5cm pieces
1 leek, cut into 2.5cm pieces
2 mushrooms, cut into 2.5cm pieces
2 tomatoes, cut into 2.5cm pieces
sprig of thyme
sprig of rosemary
1.8 litres boiling water

For the smoked bone marrow
2 x 5cm pieces of bone with marrow
a handful of pet shop hay
a handful of hickory smoking chips

continued overleaf . . .

1. Put all the vegetables with the egg whites, mince and ceps in a food processor and pulse until smooth.

2. Heat the beef mixture through gently in a wide saucepan and then add the cold beef stock.

3. Stirring constantly, bring the mixture to a gentle simmer over a high heat.

4. Once the liquid is hot and a 'raft'/crust of vegetables and mince begins to form, stop stirring.

5. Once the raft has fully formed, reduce the heat to barely a simmer and make a chimney (hole) in the middle.

6. Leave to clarify over a low heat for 1½–2 hours.

7. Remove from the heat and leave the consommé to cool, then strain through a damp muslin cloth or clean fine tea towel.

8. When reheating to serve, do not allow the liquid to boil, as this will cause it to become cloudy. Season to taste with ginger and salt.

Cut the ox cheek into four pieces and place in bowls along with the bone marrow. Pour the consommé over the top.

At the restaurant, we serve this dish over a bed of diced root vegetables, precooked lentils and barley with a drizzle of parsley oil (see page 193). Alternatively, it can be served as above – simply the cheek, bone marrow and consommé.

For the beef consommé

1 carrot, peeled and finely sliced
1 celery stick, finely sliced
1 leek, white part only, finely sliced
1 mushroom, peeled and finely sliced
1 tomato, finely sliced
3 large free-range egg whites
300g very lean beef mince
25g dried ceps
1 litre cold good-quality beef stock
ground ginger, to taste
salt

Chunky Mulligatawny

Curry! Curry! But you may think, curry soup? You can't beat this one, though. It's nearly my favourite soup apart from oxtail. My brother and sisters love this; it's a great classic and all I've done is polish it. Try it as a soup or a wintery main course.

1. Preheat the oven to 180°C/gas mark 4.

2. Heat a little vegetable oil in a flameproof casserole dish and brown the beef on all sides. Remove from the dish and set aside.

3. Add the onion, carrot and garlic to the dish and cook over a gentle heat until soft.

4. Add the curry powder, ginger and cumin and cook briefly, stirring. Add the rice, return the meat to the pan and stir together.

5. Add the hot stock and simmer for about 40 minutes until the meat is tender and the soup begins to thicken.

6. Add the parsnip and carrot and continue to simmer for about 15 minutes until the vegetables are soft.

7. Stir in the apple and simmer for 2 minutes. Season to taste with salt and black pepper and finish off with the chopped coriander and a squeeze of lime juice.

Serve in large bowls with a chunk of focaccia.

Serves 4

splash of vegetable oil
300g braising steak, cut into small dice and dusted with plain flour
1 large onion, peeled and diced
1 carrot, peeled and diced
3 garlic cloves, peeled
2 teaspoons mild curry powder
1 teaspoon ground ginger
1 teaspoon ground cumin
185g white long-grain rice
1.5 litres hot beef stock
1 parsnip, peeled and cut into large dice
1 large carrot, peeled and cut into large dice
1 Bramley apple, peeled, cored and cut into large dice
salt and freshly ground black pepper
½ bunch of coriander, chopped
½ lime, for squeezing
Focaccia, to serve (see page 173)

Easy Peasy Soup

This does exactly what it says on the tin – it's easy. Don't bother with the ham or cream if you're too lazy, but even the garnish is easy peasy.

1. Prepare the ham hock ahead of the soup – the day before if necessary. Preheat the oven to 180°C/gas mark 4.

2. Place all the ingredients in a large, lidded ovenproof pot and cover with cold water. Bring to the boil and then reduce to a simmer.

3. Cover the pot with the lid, transfer to the oven and cook for 2 hours, or until the meat falls off the bone or you can pull the bone out. (This bone is known as the mustard bone and can be cleaned and used to serve mustard).

4. Leave to cool and then pick all the meat off the bone and shred. Set aside.

1. Heat a large saucepan with a little butter or vegetable oil and sweat the onion over a gentle heat until soft, then stir in the garlic.

2. Add the peas and tarragon and then pour in the hot stock and return to the boil.

3. Whizz the mixture in a blender until smooth and then pass through a sieve. Season to taste with salt and black pepper and keep warm.

1. Whip the cream until soft peaks form, but do not overwhip, otherwise the cream will split when the other ingredients are added.

2. Whisk in the wasabi and then the mustard and finish with the chopped tarragon.

Take four bowls and garnish with the shredded ham. Spoon in a tablespoonful of the mustard cream. Pour the warm soup over the top and serve.

Serves 4

For the ham hock
1 ham hock
1 carrot, peeled
2 celery sticks
1 leek
1 onion, peeled
1 garlic clove, peeled
1 bay leaf
2 sprigs of thyme
2 branches of parsley

For the soup
knob of butter or splash of
    vegetable oil
1 onion, peeled and diced
1 garlic clove, peeled and crushed
500g frozen petits pois
½ bunch of tarragon, chopped
1 litre hot chicken or vegetable stock
salt and freshly ground black pepper

For the mustard cream
300ml whipping cream
1 teaspoon wasabi
1 heaped tablespoon coarse-grain
    mustard
½ bunch of tarragon, chopped

Leek and Potato Soup with Crème Fraîche, Crispy Barley and Chive Oil

Ahhh! Leek and potato, they're like the best of friends. I love this soup cold, but for me it's fantastic hot with crème fraîche and crunchy barley. It's great just as a big bowl of soup, but if you want to show off at a dinner party, it's also a fab way to get things going.

1. Cook the barley in a saucepan of boiling salted water for about 25 minutes, or until tender.

2. Meanwhile, preheat the oven to 110°C/gas mark ¼.

3. Drain the barley, refresh with cold water and drain again thoroughly.

4. Spread out on a baking tray and place in the oven for about 2 hours, or until completely dry.

5. Heat the oil in a large frying pan over a medium-high heat and fry the barley for about 1 ½ minutes until crispy. Remove with a slotted spoon and drain on kitchen paper.

1. Melt the butter in a frying pan and cook the onion and leeks over a gentle heat for 5 minutes until soft but not coloured.

2. Bring the water to the boil in a saucepan and then add the potatoes, bouquet garni and salt. Simmer for 25 minutes until cooked.

3. Discard the bouquet garni and stir in the onion and leeks. Whizz the mixture in a blender until smooth. Add the cream and blend again, then season to taste with ginger. Keep warm.

1. Mix the crème fraîche and cream together in a bowl.

2. Add the chives and season to taste with ginger.

Whizz the oil and chives together in a blender, then pass the mixture through a fine sieve.

Take four bowls and place a spoonful of the crème fraîche mixture in each. Sprinkle with some of the crispy barley and a drizzle of chive oil. Pour the soup over the mixture just before serving.

Serves 4

For the barley
185g pearl barley
salt
300ml vegetable oil

For the soup
15g butter
1 onion, peeled and thinly sliced
4 leeks, white parts only, sliced
2 litres water
800g firm-fleshed potatoes, peeled and chopped
1 bouquet garni – 2 sprigs of thyme and 6 branches of parsley, rolled in the green part of a leek
2 teaspoons coarse sea salt
250ml double cream
pinch of ground ginger, or to taste

For the crème fraîche
150ml crème fraîche
splash of double cream
½ bunch of chives, chopped
pinch of ground ginger, or to taste

For the chive oil
200ml light oil, such as vegetable or rapeseed
bunch of chives

Black pudding and white pudding

Black pudding and white pudding are great in all elements of cooking, unless you're making a sweet pudding! I believe the Italians use pig's blood in a dessert, but we'll leave that one for now. These are two great recipes to have a go at, that's if you're brave enough. Just follow the recipes carefully and you shouldn't have a problem. They can be served as part of a cooked breakfast/brunch, or as a starter with a poached egg. Alternatively, they can be used as a garnish for a main course of meat or fish.

Purnell's Black Pudding

1. Braise the trotter in a large saucepan of simmering slightly salted water for 2 hours, or until the meat falls off the bone. Pick off the remainder of the meat from the bone and remove and discard any sinew. Chop the trotter meat.

2. Place the diced pork fat with the onions in a heavy-based saucepan and render over a low heat for about 5 minutes until soft.

3. Cook the pearl barley in a saucepan of boiling salted water for about 15 minutes, or until soft but not mushy, then drain.

4. Pour the blood into a jug and whisk in the vinegar until the blood is no longer coagulated and is thin and free flowing with no lumps.

5. In a separate saucepan, gently roast the spice mix and mace in a little vegetable oil until fragrant, being careful not to burn the spices, as this will make the black pudding bitter.

6. Pour in the blood, whisking constantly over a low heat until just beginning to thicken and darken.

7. Remove from the heat and add the trotter meat, pork fat and onions and the pearl barley, using the residual heat to melt the trotter meat and pork fat and onions. Season with salt. The mixture is now safe to eat.

8. Divide the mixture into three and roll tightly in heatproof clingfilm, ensuring that there are no holes or air pockets.

9. Fill a saucepan large enough to accommodate the clingfilmed rolls with water and heat until the temperature reaches 80°C on a cooking thermometer. Place the rolls in the water and cook for 20 minutes, maintaining the temperature at 80°C.

10. Remove the rolls from the pan and refresh in cold water. Unwrap and slice to the desired thickness, then pan-fry in a little vegetable oil on both sides. Add a knob of salted butter to the pan and baste the black pudding with it before serving.

Makes 25 portions

1 pig's trotter
salt
300g pork back fat, diced
2 onions, peeled and finely diced
150g pearl barley
1 litre fresh pig's blood
3 tablespoons white wine vinegar
5 tablespoons Purnell's Masala Spice Mix (see page 194)
5 teaspoons finely ground mace
splash of vegetable oil, plus extra for pan-frying
knob of salted butter, to finish

Purnell's White Pudding

1. Braise the trotter in a large saucepan of simmering slightly salted water for 2 hours, or until the meat falls off the bone. Pick off the remainder of the meat from the bone and remove and discard any sinew. Chop the trotter meat.

2. Place the diced pork fat with the onions in a heavy-based saucepan and render over a low heat for about 5 minutes until soft.

3. Cook the pearl barley in a saucepan of boiling salted water for about 15 minutes, or until soft but not mushy, then drain.

4. Lay out the diced chicken and minced veal separately on a tray. Cover evenly with 1 tablespoon salt and leave for 15 minutes.

5. Place the diced chicken, whole eggs, egg white and cream in a food processor and pulse until a light mousse is formed. Do not overmix, otherwise the mixture will split.

6. Gently mix the mousse with the trotter meat, pork fat and onions, pearl barley and minced veal. Add the garlic, rosemary and thyme and season generously with salt and white pepper.

7. Divide the mixture into three and roll tightly in heatproof clingfilm, ensuring that there are no holes or air pockets.

8. Fill a saucepan large enough to accommodate the clingfilmed rolls with water and heat until the temperature reaches 80°C on a cooking thermometer. Place the rolls in the water and cook for 20 minutes, maintaining the temperature at 80°C.

9. Remove the rolls from the pan and refresh in cold water. Unwrap and slice to the desired thickness, then pan-fry in a little vegetable oil on both sides. Add a knob of salted butter to the pan and baste the black pudding with it before serving.

Makes 20 portions

1 pig's trotter
salt
300g pork back fat, diced
2 onions, peeled and finely diced
100g pearl barley
3 boneless, skinless chicken breasts, diced
500g minced veal belly
2 large whole free-range eggs
1 large free-range egg white
100ml double cream
1 garlic clove, peeled and minced
1 tablespoon rosemary leaves, finely chopped
1 tablespoon thyme leaves, finely chopped
ground white pepper
vegetable oil, for pan-frying
knob of salted butter, to finish

Egg and Black Pudding Crumble

The classic breakfast combinations are always great, and not only for breakfast but also as starters. Just like my haddock and eggs (see page 34), this is all about lifting that gooey egg yolk. In this dish I use black pudding as the texture by turning it into a delicious crumble. The freshness of the raw cauliflower and the smoky bacon purée makes this a starter or a breakfast fit for a king - or #princeofbirmingham.

1. Preheat the oven to 240°C/gas mark 9.

2. Arrange the black pudding slices on a baking tray and bake for 10-12 minutes, or until cooked through and dry. Leave the black pudding to cool slightly, then crumble into a bowl and set aside.

3. Heat a frying pan until hot, add the bacon and cook for 4-5 minutes, or until golden brown.

4. Add the chopped cauliflower and fry for 1-2 minutes. Pour in the milk and bring to the boil, then reduce the heat and simmer for 1-2 minutes. Add the bicarbonate of soda and cook for a further 4-5 minutes, or until the cauliflower is tender.

5. Whizz the cauliflower mixture in a blender until smooth, then pass through a sieve into a clean saucepan. Keep warm.

6. Whizz the olive oil and sage leaves together in a blender to a fine purée. Pass the oil through a fine sieve into a bowl.

7. Slice the remaining cauliflower florets on a mandolin. Mix the cauliflower slices, 2 tablespoons of the sage oil and a little salt together in a bowl.

8. Bring a saucepan of water to a gentle simmer and poach the duck egg yolks for 2 minutes until warmed through and starting to set but still runny. Remove with a slotted spoon and transfer to a folded piece of kitchen paper.

Spoon the cauliflower purée onto serving plates, then place the poached duck egg yolks on top. Season the yolks with salt and sprinkle over the crumbled black pudding. Top with the thinly sliced cauliflower and watercress leaves.

Serves 2

110g good-quality black pudding (see page 26), thinly sliced
75g smoked bacon, finely chopped
150g cauliflower, chopped, plus 3 medium florets
200ml full-fat milk
½ teaspoon bicarbonate of soda
200ml light olive oil
8 sage leaves
salt
2 duck egg yolks
a handful of watercress leaves

Mushroom Brioche with Duck Egg Yolk and Hollandaise

Brioche and hollandaise are French classics and pure indulgence. The addition of a rich duck egg yolk makes this dish exceptionally luxurious and not one for the faint-hearted. Have this one a couple of times a week and you'll be dragging out the treadmill or dusting off your gym membership – maybe even squeezing into that Lycra! So this comes with a health warning: eat this dish in moderation or as part of a balanced diet... or just enjoy it.

1. Beat the hen egg yolks with a splash of warm water, the anchovy essence and the vinegar in a glass bowl set over a large saucepan of water over a medium heat.

2. Slowly whisk in the clarified butter to make a smooth sauce with the consistency of mayonnaise. Season with white pepper, cover and keep warm.

3. Heat a saucepan with a little vegetable oil and sweat the shallots and garlic over a gentle heat until soft.

4. Add the mushrooms to the pan and cook until all the moisture has evaporated, then add the tarragon leaves.

5. Add the bicarbonate of soda and cook for a further 2 minutes, then stir in the hot stock.

6. Whizz the mixture in a blender to make a smooth purée, then pass through a sieve.

7. Toast the brioche on both sides and spread a little mushroom purée on each slice.

8. Bring a saucepan of water to a gentle simmer and poach the duck egg yolks for 2 minutes until warmed through and starting to set but still runny. Remove with a slotted spoon and transfer to a folded piece of kitchen paper.

9. Place a poached duck egg yolk on top of the purée on each slice of brioche, then cover with hollandaise sauce. Place under a hot grill to glaze.

Spoon the remaining mushroom purée onto each plate and place a slice of glazed brioche on top. Garnish with chervil and tarragon leaves. Season with a twist of black pepper.

Serves 4

5 large free-range hen egg yolks
1 teaspoon anchovy essence
1 tablespoon white wine vinegar
500g melted butter, clarified and cooled slightly
ground white pepper
splash of vegetable oil
2 shallots, peeled and thinly sliced
1 garlic clove, peeled and chopped
10 large field mushrooms, stalks discarded, then peeled and thinly sliced
4 sprigs of tarragon, leaves picked, plus extra to garnish
1 teaspoon bicarbonate of soda
100ml hot chicken or vegetable stock
4 slices of Brioche (see page 177)
4 duck egg yolks
freshly ground black pepper
chervil leaves, to garnish

Salad of Shrimps with Watercress, Poached Egg Yolk and Potatoes Cooked in Salted Butter

Shrimps are one of the most underestimated shellfish in the sea. These little fellas may only be small, but they pack a massive punch – the flavour is unique. You can buy shrimps peeled, but it's best to get them in the shell, and although they're a little fiddly to peel, it's well worth the effort. That's sweet coming from me, seeing as I've got nine chefs in my kitchen. I remember peeling these as a commis chef – not one of my favourite jobs, especially when you go to a nightclub after work with your fingers smelling like a fishmonger's pocket. But as a commis you are seen and not heard, unless tea is required.

1. Preheat the oven to 180°C/gas mark 4.

2. Place the potatoes in an earthenware dish and cover with the melted butter. Bake for about 15 minutes, or until soft.

3. Mix the shrimps, tarragon and mayonnaise together. Season to taste with salt and black pepper.

4. Pick the watercress leaves, dress with olive oil and season to taste with salt and black pepper.

5. Bring a large saucepan of water with the vinegar to a gentle simmer.

6. Stir the water to create a current and then crack the four eggs into the water. Cook for 1 minute, then remove from the heat and leave to stand for a further 3 minutes. Remove with a slotted spoon and transfer to a folded piece of kitchen paper.

Divide the potatoes between four serving plates and spoon the shrimp salad on top, leaving a hole in the centre of each for the poached egg. Place an egg in each hole. Garnish with the dressed watercress and season to taste with salt and black pepper. Serve with a warm muffin.

Serves 4

3 large potatoes, peeled and cut into 1cm-thick discs
200g salted butter, melted
500g cooked peeled shrimps
1 tablespoon chopped tarragon
Mayonnaise (see page 190) – enough to cover the shrimps
salt and freshly ground black pepper
200g watercress
olive oil, for dressing
1 large tablespoon distilled malt vinegar
4 large free-range egg yolks
warm muffins, to serve

Posh Sausage Roll with Winter Cabbage Salad

Whenever Chef creates something new, the ideas always start flooding in along with energy and enthusiasm; sometimes you think it's all going to get out hand! 'Quick Luke grab me this?' 'Dave where's the . . ?' Here, with just a splash of calvados, a handful of nuts, a sprinkling of spices and a few apricots Chef turned the humble sausage roll into something epic. Whenever we get a 'Eureka!' moment like this, we run around the restaurant getting staff to try whatever we have made. In this case chef was just bouncing off the walls and took samples of the sausage roll up to Purnell's Bistro. Mojitos and sausage rolls for everyone!

Dave Taylor, sous chef, Purnell's restaurant

1. Preheat the oven to 200°C/gas mark 6.

2. Heat the oil in a frying pan over a gentle heat and sweat the onion and garlic with the bacon until soft. Deglaze the pan with the Calvados, then add the apricots and mix together. Transfer the mixture to a bowl and leave to cool.

3. Place the minced pork and sausagemeat in a large bowl. Add the sage, parsley and two of the eggs, then mix together until fully combined. Add the onion mixture along with the nutmeg, ginger, salt and black pepper, breadcrumbs and pistachios. Mix together to create your filling.

4. Lay the pastry on a lightly floured surface with a short edge nearest to you. Place the filling on the pastry and form into a sausage shape across the width of the pastry partway down the length. Brush the edges of the pastry with the remaining beaten egg using a pastry brush and fold it over to create the sausage roll. Seal around the edges and brush over with egg. Using a sharp knife, slash the top of the sausage roll to create lines in the pastry.

5. Place the sausage roll on a baking tray and bake for 10 minutes. Reduce the oven temperature to 180°C/gas mark 4 and bake for a further 10-15 minutes until golden brown and cooked through.

1. To prepare the tamarind pods, remove the shells and place in a saucepan with a few tablespoons of water, bring to the boil and then simmer for about 15 minutes, or until soft. Pass through a sieve to make a purée, discarding the seeds.

2. Heat the oil in a frying pan and sweat the onion over a gentle heat until soft. Add the apple and cook for about 10 minutes until soft. Add the tamarind purée and simmer until reduced and the mixture has a sticky consistency.

3. Blanch the cabbage leaves in a large saucepan of boiling water for 2 minutes. Remove the leaves and refresh in iced water. When the leaves are cool, drain well, discard the stems and shred the leaves.

4. Melt the butter in a saucepan, add the cabbage and fry over a medium heat for about 2 minutes. Season to taste with salt and black pepper. Add the redcurrants and pomegranate seeds and stir until the currants are warm and starting to bleed.

Place a spoonful of the cabbage mixture onto each serving plate and add one of the apple and onion mixture alongside. Carve the hot sausage roll and place a piece next to the cabbage. Alternatively, the sausage roll can be served alongside roast turkey as part of the main festive event.

Serves 6-8

For the sausage roll
splash of vegetable oil
1 onion, peeled and chopped
2 garlic cloves, peeled and chopped
6 smoked streaky bacon rashers, diced
75ml Calvados
20 ready-to-eat dried apricots, diced
600g minced pork
200g sausagemeat
4 sage leaves, chopped
2 tablespoons chopped parsley
3 large free-range eggs, beaten
pinch of freshly grated nutmeg
pinch of ground ginger
salt and freshly ground black pepper
50g fresh white breadcrumbs
50g toasted shelled pistachio nuts, chopped
plain flour, for dusting
1 sheet of all-butter puff pastry, rolled ½cm
   thick, 50 x 25cm

For the winter cabbage salad
1x200g packet of dried or fresh tamarind pods
splash of vegetable oil
1 onion, peeled and chopped
1 large cooking apple, peeled, cored and
   diced
1 medium Savoy cabbage, leaves separated
knob of butter
salt and freshly ground black pepper
200g redcurrants
seeds of ½ large pomegranate

From Mum to Michelin

This dish means a lot to me. It's not only one of my signature dishes at Purnell's, it also reminds me of my childhood. My mother cooked haddock in her big flowery pan. When that particular pan came out, it was either cod's roe or haddock and eggs for tea. She would cover the haddock in milk and cook it slowly over a low heat so that the milk took on that lovely smoky fish flavour. She'd then take out the fish (which, by the way, would have been bloody overcooked), put it to one side and crack eggs into the milk to poach them. The eggs would take on the amazing flavour of the smoked haddock. The sad thing was that she would pour the milk away, but I would often take a spoon and drink the smoky liquor before she did so. That's why in my version of haddock and eggs I throw the fish away, thicken the flavoursome milk and serve it with a poached yolk.

But the big question I hear you asking is, 'Why cornflakes?' While my mother was cooking, I would be running around the garden with my siblings, feeling decidedly hungry. I would dash inside two or three times to ask for 'a piece', meaning a slice of bread. The first couple of times I'd be allowed to have one, but by the third time it would be, 'No, wait for your tea!' Gutted to be turned away, I would sneak in and pinch a pocketful of cornflakes. Then one day I put haddock, eggs and cornflakes together, and BOOM!

---

1. Put the milk in a wide, deep saucepan over a low heat and bring to a gentle simmer. Add the smoked haddock and poach for about 15 minutes until the fish begins to flake and the milk has taken on the flavour of the fish.

2. Strain the haddock through a fine sieve into a bowl, squeezing as much moisture from the haddock as possible. Transfer the milk to a clean saucepan over a low heat. Discard the haddock (or keep to use in another dish, such as kedgeree).

3. Add the xanthan gum to the milk and whisk over the heat to dissolve and thicken the milk. Add the remaining gum if required until the milk takes on the consistency of mayonnaise.

4. Pour the milk into a siphon, then place the siphon in a jug or bowl of hot water to keep the milk mixture warm.

1. Preheat the oven to 180°C/gas mark 4.

2. Mix the milk powder, sugar and salt together in a bowl.

3. Put the cornflakes into a separate bowl and sift the milk powder mixture over them. Add the melted butter and mix thoroughly.

4. Spread the cornflakes out on a baking tray lined with silicone or greaseproof paper, then bake for 10 minutes.

5. Remove from the oven and break up any lumps while still warm, then leave to cool.

6. Pulse in a food processor to break up the cornflakes.

Serves 4

For the smoked haddock foam
600ml full-fat milk
250g undyed smoked haddock fillet, skin on
½-1 tablespoon xanthan gum (available from health-food shops and online)

For the baked cornflakes
3 tablespoons milk powder
1 tablespoon caster sugar
½ tablespoon salt
60g cornflakes
3½ tablespoons melted salted butter

continued overleaf . . .

Bring a saucepan of water to a gentle simmer and poach the egg yolks for 1-2 minutes until warmed through and starting to set but still runny. Remove with a slotted spoon and transfer to a folded piece of kitchen paper.

Pipe the thickened milk from the siphon into four serving bowls to form a round. Place an egg yolk in the centre of each milk round to resemble a fried egg. Arrange or sprinkle the cornflakes over the milk, then drizzle the curry oil over the egg in a zigzag pattern.

To serve
4 large free-range egg yolks
curry oil (see page 193)

My time with Glynn

Where to begin? It's an adventure that started the day Glynn came to eat at Hibiscus Ludlow with the Simpson's team he was working with at the time. After he'd eaten, he asked me if he could do a stage with us. To me, it was a strange question, as in my eyes we were doing nothing that made it worthwhile to work for a week without pay, but I told him he was welcome to come. I still remember the day he arrived with his strange accent, and I was amazed how excited he was, how willing, how determined to be the best he could be. I said to my wife, 'This guy is completely mad, but I'd be happy to have him in my team.'

A few weeks passed and I got a call from Glynn asking me if he could have a job. We had a chat in a local pub and I tried to explain to him what life at Hibiscus was like. I told him it's hell and low wages, just to make sure he understood. I told him to think about it and come back to me. He did. To this day, I haven't worked with many chefs, but I was so happy to work with him. Sometimes, in the middle of service, we'd be in so much shite we'd start having a massive laugh - to the extent the restaurant manager would have to come in and tell us he could hear us laughing in the restaurant!

Glynn was a breath of fresh air. Nothing was a problem. Even dealing with a Canadian stagier who boiled his chef jacket in our stock pan on his day off, destroying the pan in the process! Or with someone with my hot temper. Or the long hours and the travelling back to Birmingham to make sure he kept his wife happy.

With him and the rest of my team (one other chef) we achieved two stars! The period we spent together was one of the highlights of my time in Ludlow and I know he will stay a friend forever - I love the guy!

Claude Bosi

Tomato Tartare, Basil Oil and Tomato Sorbet

Summer, summer, summertime. Even if it's pissing down with rain outside, this is sunshine on a plate. It's got acidity, sweetness and while you're eating it you won't need any sun cream... that's if you're indoors, anyway.

This dish is all about timing, when the different tomatoes are at their best – slightly squidgy overripe ones for the sorbet and the firm, plump, acidic green ones for the tartare.

Serves 4

500g very ripe tomatoes
90g Stock Syrup (see page 198)
20g liquid glucose
salt
ground ginger, to taste
6 green tomatoes
100ml olive oil
25ml Chardonnay vinegar
½ bunch of chives, finely chopped
½ bunch of basil shoots, to garnish

To serve

Basil Oil (see page 194)
black salt, for sprinkling

1. Juice the tomatoes in a juicer or whizz in a blender and pass through a fine sieve.

2. Mix the stock syrup and glucose together in a saucepan, add the juiced tomatoes and heat until completely blended. Season to taste with salt and ginger, then leave to cool.

3. Churn the tomato mixture in an ice-cream machine according to the manufacturer's instructions until it has a sorbet consistency. Transfer to a freezerproof container and store in the freezer.

4. Blanch the green tomatoes in boiling water for 12 seconds and then plunge into iced water. Peel, deseed (keep the seeds for making stock) and dice. Freeze until ready to serve, if required.

5. Mix the olive oil and vinegar together and add the chives. Toss with the diced green tomatoes and season to taste with salt and ginger.

Spoon the green tomato mixture onto serving plates or push them into a ring, depending on how posh you are! Either make scoops of the tomato sorbet or form it into quenelles by turning a heaped tablespoonful of the sorbet back and forth from the first tablespoon to a second tablespoon to create a three-sided oval. Place on top of the diced tomatoes, then drizzle with basil oil. Garnish with the basil shoots and sprinkle with black salt.

What's Next –
Hot,
Cold,
or Frozen?

Carbon Monoxide
cooking

Purnell's had only been open for a month. I had put every penny and every ounce of tears and sweat into it. Me and Kez had had to re-mortgage the house and were living on love and water. In the week, business was okay, but we really needed Fridays and Saturdays to be busy to pay for the staff and, basically, to keep us up and running. As a restaurateur, I can tell you, the shit always hits the fan on Saturdays.

This particular Saturday afternoon there was no builder or helping hand around (because they're all in the pub!) and something happened to the air extraction. We turned it on. Nothing. No idea why. To make things worse, without the extraction the gas wouldn't come on. Shit and double shit! We had 55 booked, so we needed to open. We needed the cash. I spoke to the boys and they were like, 'Chef let's do it. We don't need the extractor. We're sure chef. Yes chef, We're sure we're sure.' So I made a couple of dodgy calls to a few of my mates and got someone to come round and turn on the gas. But the instant he arrived, he said, 'You can't do this Glynn. What about fresh air?' I told him we were tough guys and to by-pass the cut-out switch. Which he did. We had the gas back and he had £50 in his pocket.

At 3 o'clock, we started prepping for the night service. People kept disappearing, and I kept finding them outside taking great lungfuls of fresh air. 'You okay?' I asked. 'Yes chef, we're fine,' they replied and jumped straight to their feet and back into the kitchen. Sandwich, my sous chef at the time, was picking the others up off the floor and saying, 'Get the fuck on with it', but the lads were coming back into the kitchen pale, white and decidedly dopey looking. I started to think we might need oxygen. But thought, fuck it, we just need to get on with it!

I got on the stove and started making sauces, but I began to feel drowsy and every time I breathed in my nose started burning. By this point the lads had started dropping to their knees. It was then that I remembered that carbon monoxide kills. Brave, or stupid, as my team were (and truly lucky!), it was time to shut down, pick up the staff, give them oxygen, cancel 55 covers and send everyone home. I was tempted to drive into a wall, as I didn't think Purnell's would be able to continue, but here we are, nearly seven years later and still going strong.

By the way, the stoves are now all electric, so no more monoxide cooking.

Beetroot Mousse with Escabeche of Vegetables

Frozen mousse? Well, it's more like a parfait really; it has a salty but sweet balance, using Parmesan to cut the sweetness. This can be made well in advance for a dinner party, or in preparation for a hot summer BBQ – just don't stick it on the grill! Served with the thinly sliced vegetables, it's a winner.

1. Melt the butter in a large saucepan, add the beetroot, vinegar and redcurrant jelly and cook over a medium heat for 2 minutes, then add the red wine and simmer until reduced by half.

2. Whizz the ingredients together in a blender to give a smooth purée.

3. Combine 500g of the beetroot purée with the olive oil, Parmesan and horseradish, and whizz together in the blender.

4. Put the mixture into a 10 x 20 x 5cm, freezerproof container and place in the freezer for about 2 hours until frozen.

1. Mix together the sunflower oil, vinegar, garlic and thyme in a saucepan and slowly warm over a low heat.

2. Add half the mixed sliced beetroot, carrot and turnip and stir well.

3. Leave to cool completely and then add the remaining root vegetables.

4. Season with salt and three or four turns of the black pepper mill.

Remove the mousse from the freezer 1 hour before serving. Form into quenelles (see page 39) or cut to size, depending on how you want to present it. Place in serving bowls and dress with the escabeche of vegetables. Watercress or rocket can be added to the presentation if you like.

Serves 4

For the beetroot mousse
75g unsalted butter
500g peeled beetroot, chopped and boiled until soft
25ml red wine vinegar
1 tablespoon redcurrant jelly
300ml red wine
60ml olive oil
40g Parmesan cheese, grated
40g creamed horseradish

For the escabeche of vegetables
170ml sunflower oil
75ml white wine vinegar
1 garlic clove, peeled and crushed
sprig of thyme
1 medium red beetroot, peeled and thinly sliced
1 medium golden beetroot, peeled and thinly sliced
1 medium candy beetroot, peeled and thinly sliced
1 large carrot, peeled and thinly sliced
1 medium turnip, peeled and thinly sliced
salt and freshly ground black pepper

Beef Carpaccio, Red Wine Octopus and Sweet and Sour Onions

Fillet is the usual choice for carpaccio of beef, but I use a single rump muscle, as I think it has a superb strong flavour. I really like marrying beef with seafood, and this meaty red wine octopus is big enough to take on the beef. The onions add a sharp freshness, while the soured cream brings it all together. I love octopus - it reminds me of holidays in Tenerife with Kerry before all the little people arrived.

1. Heat the oil in large frying pan and sear all sides of the meat - this should take four turns, 2 minutes each turn.

2. Add the butter to the pan and roll the rump in the butter to baste.

3. Remove the rump from pan and leave to cool, then roll tightly in clingfilm and freeze for 24 hours.

1. Warm the oil with the crushed peppercorns in a saucepan, then remove from the heat and leave to cool.

2. Once cool, pour into a bowl, cover and leave to steep for 24 hours.

1. Place all the ingredients in large saucepan and cover with the cold water, ensuring that the octopus is fully submerged.

2. Simmer slowly over a medium heat for 45 minutes-1 hour until the octopus is tender.

3. Leave the octopus to cool in the liquor, then remove the tentacles, discarding the remainder, and refrigerate, covered, until needed.

1. Heat the vinegar and sugar in a stainless steel saucepan until boiling and then add the onions.

2. Cook over a gentle heat for at least 20 minutes until the onions are golden. Remove from the heat and leave to cool.

1. Bring all the ingredients except the onions to the boil in a small saucepan and drop the onions into the mixture. Cook over a medium heat for 1 minute.

2. Remove from the heat and leave the onions to cool in the liquor.

1. Whip all the ingredients except the seasonings together in a bowl until stiff, then season to taste with salt and ginger.

Serves 4

For the carpaccio
50ml sunflower oil
1.5-2kg single beef rump muscle, at room temperature
25g salted butter

For the black pepper oil
200ml sunflower oil
50g crushed black peppercorns

For the red wine octopus
1 medium frozen octopus, defrosted and head discarded
500ml red wine
1 bulb of garlic, halved
about 1.2 litres cold water

For the sweet and sour onions
550ml distilled malt vinegar
500g caster sugar
5 Spanish onions, peeled, halved and finely sliced

For the pickled onions
2 juniper berries
2 black peppercorns
125ml cranberry juice
25g caster sugar
20g sherry vinegar
4 baby silverskin onions, peeled, quartered and layers separated

For the chive crème fraîche
250ml crème fraîche
15 chives, finely sliced
juice of ½ lime
25ml double cream
salt
ground ginger, to taste

continued overleaf . . .

Beef Carpaccio, Red Wine Octopus and Sweet and Sour Onions ctd

To assemble the dish

1. Allow the carpaccio to partially defrost, remove the clingfilm and slice with a sharp knife into 3-5mm slices. Place three or four slices on each serving plate.

2. Slice the octopus into medallions, but keep the ends of the curling tentacles whole, and season with olive oil and salt and black pepper. Scatter the medallions over the meat, five or six pieces per plate.

3. Place 1 teaspoon of the sweet and sour onions on the plates and scatter six to eight pieces of pickled onion across the plate.

4. Add a generous tablespoonful of the chive crème fraîche. Drizzle the dish with the black pepper oil and garnish with three or four rocket or mizuna leaves.

To serve

olive oil, for seasoning
salt and freshly ground black pepper
rocket or mizuna leaves, to garnish

The Emotions of Cheese and Pineapple 'Soixante-dix'

This is a blast from the past – a 70s classic – and an inseparable marriage. I went to a party, my son's friend's party; not rock 'n' roll, more jam roll. Kerry, Oliver, who was two, and I got there (remember it's a Sunday, my day off, i.e. hair down... well, what's left!) and I was asked if I wanted a drink. Yes please. The response I got was, 'Tea or coffee?' Pardon? Tea! WTF! I am not the two-year-old. Well, I had my tea and, slightly pissed off, stood next to a table sulking, where I started to smash cheese and pineapple on sticks down me. Wow, I loved it. So this is my version, and I'm not sulking now.

1. Preheat the oven to 150°C/gas mark 2.

2. Heat the cream and the goats' cheese in a saucepan until the cheese has melted, then simmer until fully combined. Leave to cool until just warm.

3. Whisk the eggs in a bowl and then add half the goats' cheese mixture and whisk together. Pour back into the remaining goats' cheese mixture and whisk together. Season to taste with salt and white pepper.

4. Pour into a medium square ovenproof dish lined with clingfilm and sprinkle with the Parmesan. Stand the dish in a roasting tin and fill with boiling water to halfway up the sides of the dish. Bake for 25–30 minutes.

5. Leave to cool and then cover with clingfilm and chill in the fridge.

1. Put 500ml of the pineapple juice with the sugar into a saucepan and boil until reduced by half (leaving 250ml).

2. Squeeze the excess water from the gelatine, add to the pan and stir until dissolved.

3. Stir in the remaining pineapple juice, then leave in the fridge for about 2 hours until set.

4. Remove from the fridge and transfer to a bowl. Whisk with an electric whisk until light and fluffy. Put into a 20 x 34cm, 4cm deep, baking tray and return to the fridge for at least 2 hours until reset.

1. Preheat the oven to 180°C/gas mark 4.

2. Cook the spaghetti in a saucepan of boiling salted water for 5 minutes.

3. Drain, refresh in ice-cold water, drain again and pat dry.

4. Spread out on a baking tray and bake for 8 minutes. Season to taste with salt.

1. Heat the milk in a saucepan.

2. In a separate saucepan, melt the butter and then stir in the flour.

3. Slowly add the milk, stirring constantly to ensure that there are no lumps. When all the milk has been added, you should have a smooth thick sauce.

4. Add the cheese and mix well as it melts. Stir in the mustard and cayenne, and season with salt to taste.

5. Put the sauce into a piping bag fitted with a small round piping nozzle or in a squeeze bottle.

continued overleaf . . .

Serves 4

For the cheese
300ml double cream
190g soft goats' cheese
2 medium free-range eggs
salt and ground white pepper
25g Parmesan cheese, grated

For the pineapple marshmallow
750ml pineapple juice
25g caster sugar
60g gelatine leaves, soaked in cold
  water for 10 minutes

For the crispy spaghetti
20 sticks of spaghetti
salt

For the cheese sauce
600ml full-fat milk
55g salted butter
55g plain flour
220g strong Cheddar cheese, grated
1 tablespoon Dijon mustard
¼ teaspoon cayenne pepper
salt

1. Preheat the oven to 90°C/gas mark ¼.

2. Place the pineapple on a baking tray and sprinkle with salt and black pepper and sugar to taste. Bake for 3 hours, or until crispy.

Turn the goats' cheese out of the tray, cut into 3cm squares and put two squares on each serving plate. Cut the pineapple marshmallow into 2cm squares and place a cube on top of each square of goats' cheese. Skewer the cheese and pineapple with the oven-dried spaghetti. Pierce a hole in each gougère and, using the piping bag or squeeze bottle, fill each one with warm cheese sauce. Place two gougères on each plate. Sprinkle with the dried pineapple and finish with a garnish of watercress, or, as in the picture, purée it.

For the dried pineapple
½ pineapple, peeled, cored and finely diced
salt and freshly ground black pepper
caster sugar, for sprinkling

To serve
watercress, to garnish
Gougères, to serve (see page 185)

Horseplay

Back in the day, when men were men and chefs were big, grumpy and aggressive, kitchens all had this, 'I'm bigger and harder than you' attitude, which has changed, sort of . . .

I was working in the banqueting part of the kitchen, which consisted of the Larder, the Veg, the Sauce, and Breakfast. The Sauce were okay, but Veg were another story. They were top boys. Kings of the wind-up. They always won the banter and scraps in the freezer, with the Breakfast boys coming a close second. I had just started on the Veg and for my initiation was instructed to 'take down' a Breakfast chef, meaning I had to jump on him and get him on the floor. There was little alternative but to accept the challenge.

It was a busy lunch with 400 guests, 40 large soup terrines waiting, waitresses standing to attention, and a couple of black tied head waiters at the ready. Looking around, I spotted a potential 'victim' standing by the chef's office just behind the pass. Was this my opportunity? Farley was a large guy, a very large guy, with long blonde hair. He was a gentle giant and a lovely guy, but he was a Breakfast chef. I ran, jumped on his back and attempted to wrestle him to the floor. As I was only 18 at the time and a mere weakling in comparison, this was no easy task, but I held on for dear life and eventually took him down. His hat flew off, his hair went everywhere, waitresses were laughing, and the chefs were in bits. We had a victory! As I was celebrating, I heard, 'Glenda! In my office, NOW! You, too, Farley.'

Fuck! It was Chef Wintle. Usually a calm, cool guy, he had proper lost it. His face was red and there was smoke pumping out of his ears. We were marched into the office and had the fucking hair dryer treatment. Poor Farley. I felt like shit for getting him into trouble, but as I walked back to the Veg section I was greeted with a pat on the back. I had earned my stripes.

I also received a written warning from Chef for 'extreme horseplay' – whatever that means.

Corned Beef 'OXO' with GP Sauce

GP Sauce? Well, HP Sauce used to be made in Brum and the factory was a landmark. When you drove into town, it was one of the first things you saw. Sadly, it's now gone, so this is my salute to the old sauce. And there's no better way to serve it than with homemade corned beef, perhaps in a handsome sandwich on a Sunday or in a lunchbox. I made this sauce once and gave it away in a 'GP Sauce' bottle to the food critic Matthew Fort who gave it to a friend as a gift. The next time I saw Matthew I asked him about it. His reply was, 'It exploded in my friend's cupboard!' Oh, how I slowly crawled under the nearest rock. So when you make the sauce, do keep it in the fridge.

1. Add the water, rock and pink salts and all the spices to a large saucepan and heat, stirring, until the salt has dissolved. Remove from the heat and leave to cool completely.

2. Add the flank of beef to the brine and leave to marinate in a cool place for 3 days, turning once or twice each day.

3. Preheat the oven to 180°C/gas mark 4.

4. Discard the brine and wash the flank, then place in a large, lidded ovenproof pot and cover with cold water. Bring to the boil and then reduce to a simmer.

5. Cover the pot with the lid, transfer to the oven and cook for up to 4 hours until meat is tender.

6. Scrape off the fat and set aside, then remove and discard any sinew from the meat. Chop or mince the meat.

7. Melt the beef lard in a saucepan, then add the fat from the beef and heat gently until completely melted.

8. Pass the fat through a sieve and then mix with the meat and season with salt and ginger.

9. Place the meat mixture in a shallow baking tin and pack down to form an even layer. Cover with clingfilm and leave overnight in the fridge until set.

10. Cut the corned beef into 5cm-square pieces, then roll in the OXO stock powder.

1. Heat a little vegetable oil in a saucepan and sweat the onion, garlic and chilli over a gentle heat until soft.

2. Add the mustard powder and quatre épices and cook briefly, stirring. Stir in the vinegar and orange and apple concentrates and simmer over a medium heat for 3 minutes.

3. Add the date purée, tamarind jam, sugar and glucose, then simmer for 2 minutes. Add the beef stock and simmer for 5 minutes.

4. When happy with the flavour, season to taste with salt and ginger, then stir in the potato starch paste and cook for a few minutes, stirring, until thickened.

5. Remove from the heat and leave to cool slightly and then whizz in a blender until smooth.

6. Transfer to a sterilised airtight bottle or jar and store in the fridge. It will keep for up to 2 weeks sealed. Once opened, use within 3 days.

Serve the corned beef with the chilled GP sauce.

Serves 4

For the corned beef
2 litres water
100g heavy rock salt
50g pink salt
6 cloves
6 bay leaves
5 star anise
1kg flank of beef, fat on
200g beef lard
salt
ground ginger, to taste
4 OXO beef stock cubes, crumbled
  to a powder

For the GP sauce
splash of vegetable oil
½ onion, peeled and diced
1 garlic clove, peeled and crushed
1 red chilli, chopped
1 tablespoon English mustard
  powder
1 tablespoon quatre épices
3 tablespoons distilled malt vinegar
2 tablespoons orange concentrate
1 tablespoon apple concentrate
3 tablespoons date purée (soak
  stoned dates in warm water until
  soft, then whizz with a little of
  the soaking water in a blender to
  a purée)
1 tablespoon tamarind jam (see
  page 106)
2½ tablespoons demerara sugar
1 tablespoon liquid glucose
600ml brown beef stock
salt
ground ginger, to taste
2 teaspoons potato starch, mixed
  to a smooth paste with a little cold
  water

Baked Cheddar Custard with Red Onion Salad

This is one of many recipes where I use the word custard, but this is more like a quiche consistency and I use a giant in the cheese world - British Cheddar! Cooked individually or in a family pot, this is great served hot or cold, as a starter, main course or even a cheese course.
I like it warm with brown bread or crackers, but I also have it with salad or GP Sauce (see page 53) - either way, it's delicious cheesiness.

1. Preheat the oven to 160°C/gas mark 3.

2. Put 100g of the Cheddar, the cream and the mustard in a heavy-based saucepan and heat gently until the cheese has melted and the mixture is smooth. Season to taste with salt and the ginger.

3. Beat the eggs in a bowl and then slowly whisk the cheese mixture into the eggs until well combined.

4. Strain the custard through a sieve and pour into a 17 x 22cm, 3cm deep, ovenproof dish. Sprinkle over the remaining grated Cheddar.

5. Stand the dish in a deep-sided roasting tin and pour in enough boiling water to come halfway up the sides of the dish. Bake for 40 minutes, or until the custard is set but still has a bit of a wobble.

1. Put the red onion and garlic in a salad bowl, add the raspberry vinegar, olive oil and honey and mix together. Leave to stand for 10 minutes.

2. Add the lettuce to the bowl, along with the spring onions, rocket and lime juice. Season to taste with salt and mix together thoroughly.

Serve the custard warm, with the onion salad on the table for guests to help themselves, along with warm focaccia.

Serves 4

For the Cheddar custard
170g Cheddar cheese, grated
275ml double cream
½ teaspoon prepared English mustard
salt
½ teaspoon ground ginger
4 large free-range eggs

For the onion salad
1 red onion, peeled and thinly sliced
1 garlic clove, peeled and thinly sliced
1 tablespoon raspberry vinegar
3 tablespoons olive oil
1 tablespoon runny honey
1 small Cos lettuce heart, shredded
bunch of spring onions, chopped
small bunch of rocket
juice of ½ lime
salt

To serve
warm Focaccia (see page 173)

Rabbit, Pea and Black Olive Trifle with Rabbit Lollipops

Strange, you may think, rabbit in a trifle, but it's great. This is a delicate dish that makes you smile. It's fun and a little challenging, a bit like a lovely looking... God, I sound like a dating website.

1. Preheat the oven to 200°C/gas mark 6.

2. Remove the racks, loin, kidneys, back legs and shoulders of the rabbit. Place the racks, loin and kidneys on a baking tray and roast for 2 minutes until cooked through. Remove from the oven and leave to cool slightly.

3. Roll the loins in clingfilm, making them into a sausage shape and sealing in the juices. Place the loins and a rack on a tray and leave to chill in the fridge.

4. Remove the remainder of the organs from the rabbit and the head and discard them. Put the rabbit carcass, back legs and shoulders into a large saucepan and cover with the rabbit or chicken stock. Gently simmer for about 40-60 minutes, depending on the size of the rabbit, until the meat is tender. Remove from the heat and leave to cool slightly.

5. Pick the meat off the bones of the legs and shoulders and place evenly into four trifle dishes, along with a few slices of black olive.

6. Simmer the leftover stock over a medium heat until reduced by half. Squeeze out the excess water from the gelatine and stir into the stock until dissolved, then pass through a fine sieve into a clean jug.

7. Pour the liquid into the trifle dishes, just covering the meat. Cover the dishes with clingfilm and leave in the fridge for about 3 hours until set.

1. Heat the sugar and water in a heavy-based saucepan over a medium heat until the sugar has dissolved, then increase the heat slightly and bring to the boil. Every now and then, carefully swirl the pan to even out the heat and brush the sides of the pan with a pastry brush dipped in cold water to prevent sugar crystals forming. Boil for about 3-4 minutes, or until the mixture turns to a dark golden brown caramel. Add the soy sauce and remove from the heat.

2. Line a baking tray with baking parchment. Remove the clingfilm from the chilled rabbit loins, slice them in half and trim.

3. Skewer the rabbit loins onto cocktail sticks and dip the loins in the caramel to cover. Transfer them to the lined baking tray and leave to set at room temperature for about 20 minutes.

1. Blanch the peas in a saucepan of boiling salted water for 1 minute.

2. Remove with a slotted spoon and transfer to a bowl of ice-cold water to cool. Drain well and place in a blender or food processor. Add the shallot, marjoram leaves and olive oil and pulse to a rough consistency.

3. Add 1 tablespoon of the powdered black olives and mix well, reserving the remainder.

Serves 4

For the rabbit trifle
1 whole cleaned rabbit
570ml rabbit or chicken stock
6 black olives, pitted and sliced
6g gelatine leaves, soaked in cold water for 10 minutes

For the lollipops
70g caster sugar
2 tablespoons water
splash of soy sauce

For the pea salad
200g fresh peas
salt
1 shallot, peeled and finely chopped
1 teaspoon marjoram leaves
splash of olive oil
100g black olives, pitted and baked in a low oven for 24 hours until dried, then ground in a spice grinder to a powder

continued overleaf . . .

Rabbit, Pea and Black Olive Trifle with Rabbit Lollipops ctd

1. Whip the cream in a bowl until soft peaks form, then fold in the gingerbread crumbs.

2. Season to taste with salt and black pepper, cover with clingfilm and refrigerate.

Slice the rabbit racks into cutlets and the kidneys in half. Season to taste with salt and black pepper. Remove the trifle bowls from the fridge and layer the pea custard on top of each jelly, then cover with the pea salad and the remainder of the powdered olives. Top each dish off with the cutlets, kidneys, two pea shoots and a spoonful of the gingerbread cream. Garnish the side of each bowl with a rabbit lollipop.

For the gingerbread cream
100ml whipping cream
2 tablespoons crushed gingerbread biscuits
salt and freshly ground black pepper

To serve
Pea Custard (see page 101)
8 pea shoots

Rabbit, Foie Gras and Chorizo Terrine with Raw Fennel Salad

Terrines always look and seem really difficult to make, but this one is pretty easy. Use chicken if you don't want to cook Bugsy! The soft terrine with the crisp fennel and a little spice coming from the chorizo make this a great starter.

1. Preheat the oven to 180°C/gas mark 4.

2. Put all the vegetables and garlic into a casserole dish with the thyme and rabbit legs and cover with boiling water.

3. Cover with the lid, transfer to the oven and braise for 2 hours, or until the rabbit meat is soft and falling off the bone. Remove from oven and leave the rabbit legs to cool slightly in the liquor.

4. Heat a frying pan over a medium-high heat. Cut the foie gras into 30g pieces, add to the hot pan and cook until golden brown on the underside, then turn over and cook until caramelised and golden brown on the other side, ensuring that you drain off the excess fat frequently into a separate bowl so that it doesn't burn (reserve the fat for use in other dishes). Once the foie gras is soft to the touch, remove from the pan and leave to cool for 5 minutes.

5. Wipe out the frying pan, reheat and sauté the chorizo until caramelised, then remove from the heat and drain off the fat.

6. Chop up the foie gras finely and mix with the chorizo.

7. Once the rabbit is cool enough, lift out of the liquor and pick the meat off the bones into a bowl.

8. Simmer the rabbit liquor over a medium heat until reduced to 200ml. Squeeze the excess water from the gelatine, add to the pan and stir until dissolved.

9. Add the chorizo and foie gras and rabbit liquor mixture to the rabbit meat, mix thoroughly and season to taste with salt and ground ginger.

10. Double layer cling film on a serving surface about 30cm in length. Place the meat half way down and then roll into a cylinder shape about 7cm in diameter and 30cm in length. Refrigerate for 6 hours.

1. Cut off the stalks and leaves from the fennel bulb, then cut the bulb into quarters and cut out the core from each quarter.

2. Using a mandolin or very sharp knife, thinly slice the fennel and drop into iced water.

Turn the terrine out onto a chopping board and cut to size. Drain the fennel and pat dry, then place in a bowl. Dress with the vinaigrette and season with sea salt. Place a slice of the terrine onto each serving plate, then rub with a little vinaigrette and season with sea salt. Sprinkle the fennel on and around the terrine and garnish with the red sorrel leaves.

Serves 4

For the terrine
1 onion, peeled and roughly diced
1 carrot, peeled and roughly diced
2 celery sticks, roughly chopped
3 garlic cloves, peeled and smashed
small bunch of thyme
4 rabbit legs
150g foie gras
100g cured chorizo, cut into 1cm cubes
6g gelatine leaves, soaked in cold water for 10 minutes
salt and ground ginger

For the fennel salad
1 fennel bulb
Vinaigrette (see page 190)
sea salt

small punnet of red sorrel leaves, to garnish

Foie Gras Wrapped in Kataifi with Peaches Poached in Szechuan Pepper and Almonds

Kataifi pastry is often sweetened and used in desserts, but here I have used it in a savoury way. When I worked at Simpsons, my Greek Cypriot boss chef Andreas Antona was strong on Mediterranean ingredients. We would use lots of olives and different pastries, and we would get them off a guy Andreas called The Olive. A Greek himself, The Olive would drive from London with the stuff, pop in for a quick beer and then he would be off, but not before trying to flog us some blue movies. I was more interested in the olives, obviously!

Serves 4

200ml Stock Syrup (see page 198)
2 large peaches, stoned and each cut into 8 segments
small bunch of basil, leaves picked
salt
ground ginger, to taste
4 x 35g slices of raw foie gras
3 black peppercorns, crushed
6 Szechuan peppercorns, crushed
400g packet of kataifi pastry, defrosted if frozen
splash of sunflower oil
50g butter
50g toasted flaked almonds
basil leaves, to garnish

1. Preheat the oven to 180°C/gas mark 4.

2. Pour the stock syrup into a saucepan, add the peach segments and four large basil leaves and season with a pinch of salt and ginger to taste. Very gently simmer the peaches for about 15-20 minutes until tender. Remove from the heat and leave to cool until warm.

3. Roll the slices of foie gras in the crushed black and Szechuan peppercorns and a little salt.

4. Wrap the foie gras slices individually in the kataifi pastry.

5. Heat a little sunflower oil in a frying pan, ensuring that it doesn't get too hot, and fry the foie gras wraps for 2-3 minutes on each side until a light golden brown colour.

6. Add the butter and baste the wraps in it for 30 seconds, then transfer to a baking tray. Bake for 2 minutes, then remove from the oven and leave to rest for 1 minute.

Arrange the warm peaches on serving plates and sprinkle with the chopped toasted almonds, then place the foie gras wraps on top and garnish each dish with one or two small basil leaves.

Curry Cured Salmon with Charred and Pickled Cucumber and Cucumber Sorbet

Curing, salting and preserving is a trend at the moment, but the method has been around for centuries and is pretty straightforward. I give this a little fusion, using curry powder in the curry salt mix, and serve it with an ice-cool cucumber sorbet. It's genius (big head)!

1. Prepare the salmon by removing the belly, any remaining scales and any bones (use tweezers). Wash the salmon and pat dry.

2. Mix the rock salt, sugar and curry powder together in a bowl.

3. Lay a small amount of the salt mix on the bottom of a large tray and lay the salmon on top, skin side down. Now completely cover the top of the salmon with the salt mix. Leave in the fridge for 2 days.

4. Thoroughly rinse the salt off the salmon under cold running water, pat dry and roll up in a tea towel. Cover with clingfilm and keep in the fridge until needed.

5. Cut eight 5mm-thick slices of cucumber from the peeled cucumber. Heat a frying pan over a high heat and char the cucumber very quickly, then transfer to a bowl. Cover with the vinaigrette and set aside.

6. Peel half the remaining cucumber and then whizz both halves along with the remainder of the peeled cucumber and the mint leaves in a blender. Pass through a sieve.

7. Combine the stock syrup and glucose and then add to the cucumber purée, season to taste with salt and ginger and mix together.

8. Churn in an ice-cream machine according to the manufacturer's instructions until it has a sorbet consistency. Transfer to a freezerproof container and keep in the freezer until needed.

Thinly slice the salmon and place four pieces on each serving plate. Cut the discs of charred cucumber in half and place four pieces on each plate on and around the salmon. Add a quenelle (see page 39) of sorbet and garnish with the chervil and dill leaves.

Serves 4

For the salmon
1 side of salmon, from a whole fish about 3.5–4kg
1kg rock salt
1kg caster sugar
250g curry powder
2 cucumbers, 1 peeled
3 tablespoons vinaigrette (see page 190)
10 mint leaves
90ml Stock Syrup (see page 198)
20ml liquid glucose
salt
ground ginger, to taste

To garnish
½ bunch of chervil, leaves picked
½ bunch of dill, leaves picked

Red Cabbage Mousse with Pickled Red Cabbage

Red cabbage mousse? You're probably thinking WTF? But, believe me, it's delicious and really easy to make. It's on the menu at Purnell's as it's a great dish – a little bit different, and a brilliant alternative if you don't want fish or meat as a starter. The pickled cabbage is also great served hot as a veg to go with venison or game. If you're feeling adventurous, you can mix it up and add your own spices or herbs to the cabbage, but it's a perfect little winter salad as it is, and my little curve ball.

Serves 4

1. Heat the butter in a large saucepan and sweat the onion over a gentle heat until soft.

2. Add the cabbage and cook for 5 minutes, then add the milk and simmer over a medium heat until reduced by half.

3. Whizz the cabbage mixture in a blender and then pass through a sieve into a clean saucepan.

4. Squeeze out the excess water from the gelatine, add to the cabbage purée and heat, stirring, until dissolved. Pour into a medium-size plastic tub, cover with clingfilm and leave in the fridge for 2-3 hours until set.

For the mousse
25g salted butter
½ red onion, peeled and diced
200g red cabbage hearts, finely chopped
625ml full-fat milk
12g gelatine leaves, soaked in cold water for 10 minutes

1. Sprinkle the cabbage with the salt in a colander and leave to stand for 3 hours, then rinse off the salt under cold running water and put into a non-reactive bowl.

2. Combine the vinegars, red wine and sugar in a large saucepan (not aluminium) and simmer over a medium heat until reduced by half.

3. Grind all the spices together in a food processor, then add to the vinegar mixture and leave to infuse for 5 minutes. Pass through a sieve and discard the solids.

4. Pour over the cabbage and store in the fridge until needed.

For the pickled red cabbage
700g red cabbage, finely shredded
160g coarse sea salt
540g distilled malt vinegar
280ml white wine vinegar
280ml balsamic vinegar
800ml red wine
500g caster sugar
2 star anise
6 dried bay leaves
6 cloves
2 tablespoons black peppercorns
2 tablespoons pink peppercorns
2 cinnamon sticks
2 whole dried chillies

Drain the liquid from the pickled cabbage and arrange the cabbage on serving plates. Turn the mousse out from the moulds and place on top of the cabbage. Garnish with the watercress leaves.

bunch of watercress, leaves picked, to garnish

Fins
Shells
and Tentacles

Lobster,
steak tongs
and a sous chef

As a young apprentice many years ago – back when I had long hair and I was slightly better looking – I worked at a large hotel with a massive banqueting suite. It was a really lively kitchen, with loads of chefs and massive fridges and freezers. It was coming up to the start of the motor show at the NEC, a massive exhibition that not only took over the hotel but also Birmingham.

We were all called in on the Sunday, well all the juniors were, to prep for the big dinner. Sunday shifts were pretty shit and I had been out the night before so I was slightly hungover too. Lobsters. Hundreds of them. What a ball ache! You need to break them all down, tie the tail to a spoon to keep them straight (this makes them easier to carve), cook them all off, refresh them and then get the meat out of the shells. So I cracked on for a good couple of hours; I proper smashed it, but it got a bit boring.

It was then we noticed a certain sous chef in the kitchen office, one of the easy-going ones, doing the rota and paper work. This guy was a little frightened of lobsters, so a plan was formed. Next thing he knew, six or so of us were in the office dragging him out screaming and shouting. 'You wait till I tell the fucking chef!' We pulled him into the deep freezer, pinned him to the floor, ripped his jacket off and left him with just a necktie on. Brilliant! We all piled on top of him, and showed him the lobster with the elastic bands around its claws removed. He was still screaming and swearing as we started to walk the lobster down his chest towards his tackle. We then removed his trousers, revealing his baggy shorts, and pinned him to the freezing cold floor. Not being able to see what was happening, he cried out, 'NO! NO!', and 'Stop! Stop! Get it off!' as he felt a pinch and a nip to his shrunken tackle. We all jumped up and ran for our lives. We couldn't stop laughing; it was so funny. It was then we revealed the real cause of the 'pinch' by waving the steak tongs at him from across the kitchen. We just heard, 'You bastards!'

The lobster was cooked and eaten by happy customers. The tongs were cleaned and used, and the sous chef was well and truly pissed off.

Crab Salad with Lemon Mayonnaise, Smoked Paprika Honeycomb and Pickled Apples

Love it! Love it! My absolute favourite crab salad and such a pleasure to eat. The honeycomb with the smoked paprika makes a great combo, not just in terms of flavour but texture too. As a child, my mum would take us to the local fair where, as a treat, us kids would have a bag of honeycomb, which we called cinder toffee, to share. Although it's a pudding-type thing, I like to use honeycomb to sweeten or give a little bitterness to savoury dishes. It also has an amazing crunch.

1. Heat a little vegetable oil in a large saucepan and sweat the vegetables over a gentle heat until softened.

2. Add the thyme, bay leaves, peppercorns and the water and bring to the boil.

3. Drop in the crab and cook for 12 minutes, then remove with a slotted spoon and, protecting your hands from the heat, take off the claws and drop straight into iced water to refresh.

4. Return the body to the pan for a further 8 minutes, then remove with a slotted spoon and drop into the iced water.

5. Crack the claws and body, remove all the meat and refrigerate.

1. Whisk the egg yolks, mustard and vinegar together in a bowl.

2. Very slowly and gradually whisk in the oil until the mixture has emulsified and thickened, ensuring that the mixture does not split. If too thick, thin down with a splash of water.

3. Beat in the lemon juice to taste and season to taste with salt. Add the picked crab meat to the mayonnaise.

1. Mix the sugar and vinegar together in a bowl until the sugar dissolves.

2. Add the apple to the vinegar mixture and mix well.

1. Put the sugar, honey, glucose and water into a saucepan and boil until the liquid reaches 150°C on a sugar thermometer. (The liquid will double in volume, so make sure you use a big enough pan.)

2. Add the bicarbonate of soda and quickly whisk to combine. The mixture will rise up in the pan when the bicarb is added, so be careful. Immediately pour the mixture into a non-stick baking tray.

3. Sprinkle all over with the paprika and leave to cool at room temperature, uncovered.

Spoon the crab mixture evenly onto serving plates. Scatter the pickled apples over and around the crab mixture. Grate the paprika honeycomb over the dish, dust with paprika and garnish with four or five sorrel leaves.

Serves 4

For the crab salad
splash of vegetable oil
1 carrot, peeled and chopped
1 leek, chopped
1 onion, peeled and chopped
2 celery sticks, chopped
sprig of thyme
2 bay leaves
4 white peppercorns
5.6 litres water
1 medium live cock crab (1–1.5kg)

For the lemon mayonnaise
2 large free-range egg yolks
1 tablespoon Dijon mustard
1 tablespoon Chardonnay vinegar
260ml sunflower oil
juice of ½ lemon
salt

For the pickled apples
30g caster sugar
30ml cider vinegar
1 large apple (such as Granny Smith), peeled, cored and sliced

For the honeycomb
200g caster sugar
35g runny honey
70ml liquid glucose
2 tablespoons water
10g bicarbonate of soda
1 tablespoon smoked paprika

To garnish
paprika
bunch of sorrel

Lobster Pistachio Kebabs with Coconut Risotto

I had a chance to work in the South of France, like a busman's holiday, at the three-star Le Jardin des Sens in Montpellier, and it was brilliant. I laboured hard all day and drank beer at night with a pastry chef called Ginge – three guesses as to what colour his hair was. Anyway, I saw this technique with lobster at Le Jardin, and I just loved how simple but how special it was, so here is my cheeky version.

1. Pre-soak eight 20cm wooden skewers in cold water for about 30 minutes.

2. Bring a large saucepan of salted water to the boil. When the water is boiling, stab the lobster in the back of the head with the tip of a large, heavy sharp knife, which will kill it instantly. Separate the claws and tail from the body – keep the body for making stock for other dishes, freezing it if necessary. Add the tail to the boiling water and cook for 3 minutes. Remove with a slotted spoon and drop straight into iced water to refresh.

3. Drop the claws into the boiling water and cook for 5-6 minutes, depending on their size. Remove and drop straight into the iced water.

4. Remove the meat from the shells, keeping the shells for making stock.

5. Cut the meat into 2cm pieces and push onto the soaked skewers - four or five pieces on each. Keep the lobster trimmings to add to the risotto.

6. Whisk the egg whites lightly in a bowl until frothy.

7. Roll the lobster meat on the skewers in the egg whites until the meat is completely coated.

8. Spread out the pistachios on a tray and roll the meat over the nuts, again until completely coated.

9. Heat a little vegetable oil in a frying pan over a medium heat and fry the lobster kebabs, turning frequently, for about 8 minutes until light brown and crispy all over.

1. Put the coconut milk and lime leaves into a saucepan and simmer over a medium heat until reduced by a third. Set aside.

2. In a separate saucepan, cook the rice in boiling salted water for 6-7 minutes until soft but with a little bite. Drain and rinse the rice under cold running water, then pat dry and set aside.

3. Heat a little vegetable oil in a saucepan and sweat the shallot and garlic over a gentle heat until soft. Add the rice and stir to coat in the mixture.

4. Gradually add the coconut milk to the rice a ladleful at a time, stirring over a medium heat until almost all is absorbed before adding more. When the mixture begins to thicken, add the lobster trimmings, mint and Parmesan. Season to taste with salt, ginger and lime juice.

Serve the risotto in bowls with the lobster kebabs.

Serves 4

For the lobster kebabs
salt
1kg live lobster
300g shelled pistachio nuts, finely ground
3 large free-range egg whites
splash of vegetable oil

For the coconut risotto
400ml can full-fat coconut milk
2 kaffir lime leaves
200g Arborio rice
salt
splash of vegetable oil
1 shallot, peeled and finely chopped
1 garlic clove, peeled and finely chopped
lobster trimmings (see above)
12 mint leaves, finely shredded
1 tablespoon finely grated Parmesan cheese
ground ginger, to taste
juice of ½ lime

Spiced Potted Shrimps with Coriander and Cucumber

I like to look at some classics and give them a makeover. I don't like to kill the original, but sometimes a revamp can make it happen and this really works for me – a Brummie fusion with shrimps.

1. Melt the clarified butter with all the spices in a saucepan. Add the shrimps and stir over a gentle heat – don't let the shrimps get too hot, otherwise they will become tough.

2. Divide the mixture between four small Kilner jars and seal, then refrigerate. Take out of the fridge an hour or so before serving.

3. Peel the cucumber, then split in half lengthways. Cut off the seedy centre from each cucumber half, then slice into half-moon shapes.

4. Mix the olive oil and vinegar together to make a dressing and then dress the cucumber and season to taste with salt and white pepper.

Serve the potted shrimps, garnished with coriander shoots, with warm toast.

Serves 4

225g clarified butter
¼ teaspoon ground ginger
¼ teaspoon paprika
¼ teaspoon mild curry powder
¼ teaspoon Purnell's Masala Spice Mix (see page 194)
500g freshly boiled shrimps, peeled
½ cucumber
50ml light olive oil
1½ teaspoons white wine vinegar
salt and ground white pepper
coriander shoots, to garnish
warm toast, to serve

Service with a Smile

At my first hotel job, when the French restaurant closed for the summer the staff had to cover in other restaurants. One of these was The Boulevard, which had a massive carvery where we had to serve the guests. Some of the chefs loved it, others not so much. Myself, I wasn't too fussed.

One lunchtime, the female chef at the carvery had a face like a smacked arse, and was not happy at all. 'I'm a chef, not a bloody waiter!'

A suited man walked up holding a plate with an avocado filled with prawns on it.
'Erm, chef,' he said. No reply.
'Excuse me chef,' he said again. She turned around, frowned at him and said, 'Yes sir?'
'My avocado is rock hard,' he said.
She looked at the plate, looked at him and said, 'Pass it here.'

She waved her hand over the plate, in the style of Paul Daniels, said 'ABRACADABRA', passed the plate back, turned and walked away. Leaving the customer with his mouth open, gazing at me with my mouth open. The look on his face was brilliant.

Crispy Pork-covered Squid with Chilli Sauce
My last supper!

This would be my last supper. Squid has always been a favourite of mine but this is mega squid. With chilli and wrapped in crispy pork and deep fried this would be my Heaven before Heaven.

1. Heat the vegetable oil in a deep-fat fryer or deep saucepan until it reaches 180°C.

2. Mix the ginger, paprika and garam masala together in a bowl.

3. Put the flour in a separate bowl, the eggs in another bowl and the airbag in a fourth bowl.

4. Roll the squid rings in the spices, next in the flour, then the egg and finally the airbag. Set aside until ready to fry.

5. Heat the sugar in a heavy-based saucepan until melted and lightly coloured. Add the vinegar or dashi and simmer until reduced by a third.

6. Add the chopped chilli, garlic, fresh ginger, lemongrass and chilli powder to the pan and boil until a light coating consistency is reached.

7. Stir in the soy sauce and lemon juice and then remove from the heat. Add the chopped coriander and keep warm.

8. Deep-fry the squid for about 1–2 minutes until golden brown and crispy. Drain from the oil and season with a little salt.

Serve the squid hot with the chilli sauce, garnished with coriander leaves and lime wedges.

Serves 4

vegetable oil, for deep-frying
½ teaspoon ground ginger
½ teaspoon paprika
½ teaspoon garam masala
100g plain flour
2 large free-range eggs, beaten
120g airbag (dried, powdered pork skin, available from good delicatessens, or online)
4 x 200g squid tubes, cleaned and cut into rings
200g caster sugar
200ml white wine vinegar or dashi
1 medium-hot red chilli, chopped
2 garlic cloves, peeled and finely chopped
½ teaspoon chopped fresh ginger
1 lemongrass stalk, crushed and chopped
pinch of chilli powder
splash of dark soy sauce
squeeze of lemon juice
½ bunch of coriander, leaves picked and chopped, plus extra leaves to garnish
salt
lime wedges, to garnish

Pan-fried Sea Bass 'Heaven and Earth' with Caviar Cream

This recipe title is me being romantic: the apple falls from heaven and the potato is brought up from the earth. But fuck romance – they just work. The sharp apples on the buttery potato are a great marriage, and with the fresh bass and luxury caviar it's a living dream.

1. Preheat the oven to 180°C/gas mark 4.

2. Cook the diced potatoes in a large saucepan of boiling salted water for about 10 minutes until soft but not mushy, then drain well.

3. In a separate large saucepan, melt a knob of the butter and sweat the apple over a gentle heat until soft. Add the sage, potatoes and another 50g of the butter and beat together.

4. Grease four 7cm ring moulds about 3cm deep with some of the remaining butter. Heat a little vegetable oil in a large frying pan. When hot, place the moulds in the pan and spoon the potato mixture inside, pushing it down inside the moulds so that it is level. Fry on each side for about 3 minutes until golden brown. Keep warm.

5. Pour the white wine into a saucepan and simmer over a medium heat until reduced by half. Add the cream and continue to reduce until the mixture coats the back of a spoon.

6. Leave the cream mixture to cool slightly, then add the caviar and stir well. (Ensure that the cream mixture isn't too hot, otherwise it will cook the caviar and make it hard.) Season to taste with a squeeze of lemon and salt. Keep warm.

7. Dust the sea bass fillets lightly with the flour. Heat an ovenproof frying pan until hot, add a little vegetable oil and cook the sea bass fillets, skin side down, for 3-4 minutes until the skin is crisp and golden brown.

8. Transfer the pan to the oven and cook for a further 2 minutes. Remove from the oven and turn the fillets over. Add the remaining knob of butter and baste the fish with the juices. Season to taste with salt.

Spoon the cream onto serving plates and then place the 'heaven and earth' from the ring moulds next to the cream. Place the sea bass fillets on top.

Serves 4

3 medium potatoes, peeled and diced
salt
150g butter
1 large cooking apple, peeled, cored and diced
6 large sage leaves, cut into strips, plus extra for garnishing
vegetable oil, for pan-frying
150ml white wine
300ml double cream
1 heaped tablespoon caviar
squeeze of lemon juice
4 x 125g sea bass fillets, pin-boned (see page 79) and skin lightly scored
1 tablespoon plain flour, for dusting

Mackerel and Potato Pakoras

Indian starters or side dishes make great little middle courses or are fantastic for a banquet. I love pakoras. They remind me of the times when Kez and I were proper broke and lived in a tumble-down cottage with no heat except for a fire in the living room. On Sundays, we had just enough money for a takeaway and would order five starters that we called 'millions of starters', which we would then wash down with a cheeky bottle or two - with the result that we'd be empty-pocketed for the rest of the week. That's rock 'n' roll.

1. Pin-bone the mackerel fillets: remove the line of bones down the centre of the fillets with tweezers.

2. Mix together the rock salt, sugar, coriander and cumin seeds and ginger, and spread half the mixture on a tray. Place the mackerel fillets on top, then cover with the remainder of the salt mixture.

3. Leave for 5 minutes, then remove the mackerel fillets, rinse off thoroughly under cold running water and dry with a clean tea towel. Cut into 1cm dice.

4. Mix the flours and lemon juice together in a bowl, then beat in enough water to thicken the mixture so that it coats the back of a spoon. Season with salt.

5. Add the masala spice mix, chilli, diced cooked potato, chopped coriander and diced mackerel.

6. Heat 2cm of vegetable oil in a deep frying pan over a medium heat, or use a deep fat fryer. Drop tablespoonfuls of the mixture into the hot oil and fry for 3-4 minutes until golden.

Serve the pakoras warm with the minted yogurt.

Serves 4

2x200g mackerel fillets
300g rock salt
50g caster sugar
1 teaspoon coriander seeds
1 teaspoon cumin seeds
1 teaspoon ground ginger
125g gram flour
25g self-raising flour
squeeze of lemon juice
salt
1 teaspoon Purnell's Masala Spice
  Mix (see page 194)
1 red chilli, deseeded and diced
1 peeled and cooked medium
  potato, diced
½ bunch of coriander, chopped
vegetable oil, for deep-frying
natural yogurt mixed with shredded
  mint, to serve

Monkfish Masala with Red Lentils, Pickled Carrots and Coconut Garnish

Who doesn't like monkfish?? Really, it's meaty in a delicate fish form and is used all over; with olives, with bacon, the lot. But it's big and can hold itself too. The next question; who doesn't like curry?? So, monkfish and curry - two of my favourites together. This dish works as a starter or as the main event, also (now this is swearing or blasphemy) the lentils can work as a vegetarian option.

1. Preheat the oven to 90°C/gas mark ¼, or the lowest setting.

2. Spread the carrot slices out on a baking tray and put in the oven overnight, or for 8 hours, until dried out. Pack the carrot slices into a sterilised airtight jar.

3. Mix all the spices and salt with enough vegetable oil to cover the carrots, pour over the carrots in the jar and seal. Leave for a couple of weeks (longer if you can) in a cool place before serving.

1. Sprinkle the salt over the monkfish fillets and leave for 5-6 minutes to draw out the moisture.

2. Rinse the salt off thoroughly under cold running water. Wrap the monkfish in a clean tea towel and leave overnight in the fridge.

3. Spread out the spice mix on a plate and roll the monkfish fillets in the mixture. Seal each fillet in a vacuum food bag and cook for 11 minutes in a water bath at 63°C. Alternatively, wrap each fillet in heatproof clingfilm. Heat a saucepan of water until it reaches 63°C on a cooking thermometer, add the wrapped fillets and cook for 11 minutes, keeping the temperature constant.

4. Melt the butter in a frying pan over a medium heat until foaming. Remove the fish from the bags or clingfilm and then sear on each side for 2-3 minutes until golden brown and crisp all over.

Serves 4

For the pickled carrots
3 carrots, peeled and sliced
1 tablespoon fenugreek seeds
1 teaspoon ajwain seeds
1 teaspoon black mustard seeds
½ teaspoon onion seeds
1 teaspoon cumin seeds
⅓ teaspoon chilli flakes
1 teaspoon salt
vegetable oil - enough to cover
  the carrots

For the monkfish
300g rock salt
4 x 130g monkfish fillets
4 tablespoons Purnell's Masala Spice
  Mix (see page 194)
25g butter

continued overleaf

Monkfish Masala with Red Lentils and Pickled Carrots ctd

1. Heat a splash of vegetable oil in a saucepan and sweat the onion over a gentle heat for 4-5 minutes until softened. Stir in the curry powder, then add the lentils, stir well and cover with the stock. Simmer for 10-15 minutes, or until the lentils are tender.

2. When the lentils are cooked, stir in the chilli, coriander and lime juice and season to taste with salt. Set aside.

1. Pour the coconut milk into a saucepan and add the lime leaf and salt. Simmer over a medium heat for about 15-20 minutes until reduced by half.

2. Heat a frying pan until hot and toast the coconut strips for about 2 minutes until golden brown and fragrant.

Spoon the lentils onto each serving plate. Carve each monkfish fillet in half and place one piece of monkfish on top of the lentils and the other piece next to them. Drizzle over a bit of the reduced coconut milk, then garnish with the toasted coconut strips, pickled carrots and coriander shoots.

For the red lentils
splash of vegetable oil
½ onion, peeled and chopped
1 tablespoon mild curry powder
225g dried red lentils
500ml chicken stock
½ red chilli, finely chopped
2 heaped tablespoons chopped
  coriander
juice of ½ lime
salt

For the coconut garnish
400ml can full-fat coconut milk
1 kaffir lime leaf
pinch of salt
½ fresh coconut, flesh only, thinly
  sliced into strips on a mandolin

To serve
coriander shoots (sprouted coriander
  seeds), to garnish

Brill with Toffee and Cumin Carrots

A traditional way of cooking fish is in milk, using haddock or sometimes plaice. So again I'm giving a classic a makeover by poaching brill, which is a lovely fish, rather than the more expensive turbot, in coconut milk. Used to glaze the fish, the coconut milk gives it a rich, creamy taste with a clean finish and goes great with the sweet and slightly spiced toffee carrots.

Cooking the fish slowly enables you to prep as it cooks, therefore not stressing you out but just making it happen.

Mix all the ingredients together thoroughly in a bowl until you have a smooth dressing. Set aside.

1. Pour the coconut milk into a large saucepan, then stir in the garam masala, ajwain seeds and curry powder.

2. Bring the liquid to a gentle simmer over a medium heat. Lay the brill fillets in the simmering coconut milk and cook gently for 3–4 minutes.

3. Remove from the heat, but leave the fish in the coconut milk to keep warm.

1. Tip the sugar into a heavy-based frying pan and leave it to melt, undisturbed, over a medium heat.

2. When it starts to bubble and turn golden, drop in the butter cubes and cumin and, holding the pan handle, carefully swirl the mixture until it turns to a toffee.

3. Stir in the wide carrot strips until they are coated in the toffee, then mix in the passion fruit flesh and seeds.

Using a fish slice, remove the fish fillets from the coconut milk and transfer to serving plates. Season them with the rock salt and ginger. Lay the toffee carrot strips alongside the fish, then finish the fish and toffee carrots with the carrot vinaigrette. Garnish with small herb and salad leaves.

Serves 4

For the carrot vinaigrette
8 tablespoons olive oil
2 teaspoons aged balsamic vinegar
2 large carrots, peeled and shredded into thin strips
zest of 1 lemon

For the fish
600ml canned full-fat coconut milk
pinch of garam masala
pinch of ajwain seeds
1 teaspoon curry powder
4 x 150g brill fillets
pinch of rock salt
2 pinches of ground ginger

For the toffee carrots
50g caster sugar
25g salted butter, cubed
1 teaspoon ground cumin
2 carrots, peeled and cut into wide strips using a mandolin or vegetable peeler
1 large passion fruit, halved and flesh and seeds scooped out

small herb and salad leaves, to garnish

Salad of English Asparagus and Scallop with Cockle Tartare and Mint Oil

Tartare sauce is a perfect sauce for fish. Lots of acidity and crunch from the gherkins and capers, cucumber adding freshness and chilled sea-salty cockles make this a tartare sauce on steroids. A big rule is not to put mint and seafood together, but here it's the asparagus that becomes the middle guy to bring it all together. And scallop? Well, the scallop is mustard with it all.

1. Whisk the egg yolks, mustard and vinegar together in a bowl.

2. Very slowly and gradually whisk in the oil until the mixture has emulsified and thickened, ensuring that the mixture does not split. If too thick, thin down with a splash of water.

3. Add the capers, gherkins, cucumber and cockles to the mixture, reserving a few cockles for garnish.

1. Blanch the asparagus in a saucepan of boiling salted water for about 2 minutes until just cooked but still crunchy. Remove from the water and refresh in iced water, then drain well.

2. Whizz the mint and 150g sunflower oil together in a blender until smooth, then pass through a sieve.

3. Heat a splash of sunflower oil in a frying pan until hot and fry the scallops on each side for 45 seconds. Add the butter to the pan and baste the scallops, then season to taste with salt.

4. Season the asparagus with the mint oil and salt and black pepper to taste.

Dress each serving plate with the asparagus, scallops and cockle tartare, and garnish with the watercress and rocket leaves. Scatter the reserved cockles across the plates and finish with a drizzle of mint oil.

Serves 4

For the cockle tartare
2 large free-range egg yolks
1 teaspoon Dijon mustard
1 teaspoon white wine vinegar
275g sunflower oil
25g capers, chopped
25g gherkins (cornichons), chopped
20g cucumber, diced
20–30 cooked cockles

For the salad
6 English asparagus spears, trimmed
salt
30g mint leaves
150g sunflower oil, plus an extra
  splash for cooking the scallops
4 large scallops, shelled and cleaned
knob of butter
freshly ground black pepper

To garnish
½ bunch of watercress, leaves picked
2 handfuls of rocket leaves

Turbot with Scorched Lettuce, Fondue of Onion and Crème Fraîche

This could be a dish for a dinner party or a BBQ. The turbot kept on the bone on the barbecue would be amazing, and the crisp Cos lettuce thrown over the hot grill is class too. Onion cooked down in butter and then mixed with crème fraîche sounds rich, and it is, but it has a warm acidity to it that marries well with the fish and scorched lettuce. All you need is a massive glass of chilled white wine, about the size of a bottle.

1. Preheat the oven to 200°C/gas mark 6.

2. Dust the turbot fillets with the flour, shaking off the excess, then rub with the olive oil.

3. Heat an ovenproof frying pan until hot and fry the turbot fillets on each side for about 3 minutes until golden brown. Transfer the pan to the oven and cook for a further 4–5 minutes until the fish is just cooked through.

1. Heat a frying pan until medium hot, add the butter and sliced onions and cook over a medium heat for about 15 minutes until soft.

2. Add the crème fraîche and spring onions and stir through. Season to taste with black pepper and then add the chives. Remove from the heat and set aside until needed.

1. Blanch the leeks in a saucepan of boiling salted water for 2–3 minutes. Remove with a slotted spoon and refresh in iced water, then drain well.

2. Scorch the lettuce leaves with a kitchen blowtorch or in a hot frying pan or under a hot grill and then season to taste with salt and black pepper. Mix with the watercress and blanched baby leeks.

3. Whisk the vinegar, half the lemon juice and the olive oil together in a bowl to make a vinaigrette. Season to taste with salt and black pepper.

Remove the turbot from the oven. Add the knob of butter and the remaining lemon juice from the lettuce to the pan and then baste the fish with the juices. Spoon some of the onion fondue onto each serving plate and then top with a turbot fillet. Dress the lettuce, watercress and leeks with the vinaigrette and arrange around the turbot.

Serves 4

For the turbot
4 x 150g turbot fillets
50g plain flour, for dusting
1 tablespoon olive oil
knob of butter

For the onion fondue
50g butter
2 large onions, peeled and sliced
300g crème fraîche
4 medium spring onions, shredded
freshly ground black pepper
½ bunch of chives, finely chopped

For the scorched lettuce
8 whole baby leeks
salt
8 Cos lettuce leaves
freshly ground black pepper
bunch of watercress
1 tablespoon white wine vinegar
juice of ½ lemon
4 tablespoons olive oil

One-pot Pollack with Chorizo, Butter Beans and Goats' Cheese

I love cooking but, like most people, I hate washing up. As a commis chef, if the porter didn't come in, it meant that it was my job - moody, but that's the kitchen culture. As a commis chef, if I was given half a chance to fuck about I would take it. Whenever I did, though, I'd hear Big Roger (the late Roger Kendrick, my first head chef) shout, in a bit of a stutter, 'Glenda, I can't hear you moving!', and I would pop my head up and shout, 'Yes chef!'
Washing up for this dish is easy, as it's a one-pot wonder. Sorry, I can't hear you moving!

Serves 4

4 x 140g skinless pollack fillets, pin-boned (see page 79)
25g plain flour, for dusting
splash of vegetable oil
400g can butter beans, rinsed and drained
½ Spanish cooking chorizo, cut into strips
200ml hot chicken stock
500g baby spinach
100g goats' cheese
2 teaspoons unsalted butter
crusty bread, such as bloomer or French baguette, to serve

1. Dust the pollack fillets with the flour, shaking off any excess.

2. Heat a frying pan until hot, add a little vegetable oil and fry the fish fillets for 3-4 minutes until golden brown. Carefully turn the fish over and fry for a further 1-2 minutes, or until golden brown and just cooked through (the fish should be opaque all the way through).

3. Add the butter beans and chorizo to the pan, then the stock and cook for 4 minutes to heat through.

4. Add the spinach, goats' cheese and butter to the pan and cook until the cheese is melted.

Place each fish fillet in a shallow serving bowl and spoon the butter bean mixture around. Serve with some crusty bread.

Roast Cod with Wild Horseradish

I did a demo with a great mate of mine, Nathan Outlaw, in front of 300 or so chefs at a conference. The first demo was on foraging, which went on for an hour and bored the bollocks off everyone. When it was time for me and Big Nape Dog to do our stuff they were all half asleep. So I start with a cock joke, which went down well and got their attention. Then I broke into a little rant about foraging in city centres and shouted, 'You'll find only two things in the city, dog shit and crisp wrappers!'

Now, after having been taken on a foraging tour, I have discovered there are little treasures to be found, like wild horseradish. It's smoother and sweeter than the home-grown stuff and is great with white fish and a variety of meats.

1. Mix the salt, sugar and lemon zest and juice together. Rub the mixture into the cod in a non-reactive dish, coating it completely, then cover with clingfilm and leave to marinate in the fridge for 6 hours.

2. When ready to cook, rinse off the marinade from the cod under cold running water, pat dry and lightly dust with flour. Set aside.

3. Heat a tablespoon of the olive oil in a saucepan and sweat the shallot and horseradish over a gentle heat for about 2-3 minutes until softened. Add the white wine to the pan and cook until most of it has evaporated, then stir in the cream. Simmer until the sauce thickens enough to coat the back of a spoon. Strain through a fine sieve and set aside.

4. Heat the remaining olive oil in a frying pan and fry the cod, skin-side down, for 3-4 minutes until the skin is crisp and golden brown. Carefully turn the fish over and cook for a further 2-3 minutes, or until just cooked through.

Spoon some of the horseradish sauce onto serving plates and place the fish alongside. Garnish with sakura and mizuna leaves.

Serves 4

200g rock salt
200g caster sugar
zest and juice of 1 lemon
2 x 170g cod fillets, skin on
plain flour, for dusting
2 tablespoons olive oil
1 shallot, peeled and chopped
1 medium wild horseradish root,
  peeled and grated
100ml white wine
200ml double cream
sakura and mizuna leaves, to garnish

Pan-fried Roasted Cod with Confit Lemon and Zhoug 'My Way'

Zhoug is a Middle Eastern sauce/salsa or flavoured oil. It's great, but I have added a few Indian spices, which works well with fish or some lighter meats. Sweet lemon plays a proper part here, not just as the support act.

1. Preheat the oven to 180°C/gas mark 4.

2. Mix the water and sugar together in a saucepan over a medium heat until simmering. Add the basil and the lemon slices and simmer for 5 minutes. Remove from the heat and set aside.

3. Crush the black peppercorns and caraway, cardamom, mustard and ajwain seeds with a pestle and mortar.

4. Whizz the coriander, chillies, garlic, a drizzle of olive oil, a splash of water, a pinch of salt and the crushed spices in a blender to form a green paste. This is the zhoug. Add more olive oil if needed to achieve a mayonnaise consistency.

5. Heat an ovenproof frying pan until hot, add a little vegetable oil and fry the cod fillets on each side for about 3 minutes until golden brown. Transfer the pan to the oven and cook for a further 4 minutes.

6. Remove the pan from the oven – the fish should be golden and moist. Add the butter to the pan, turn the fish over and then baste with the juices. Season to taste with salt and ginger.

Spoon the zhoug onto serving plates and then place the fish alongside. Dress the fish with the lemon slices, drizzle with the lemon liquid and garnish with picked coriander leaves and a crack of the black pepper mill.

Serves 4

150ml water
50g caster sugar
a handful of basil leaves with stalks
1 lemon, sliced as thinly as possible
1 teaspoon black peppercorns
1 teaspoon caraway seeds
seeds of 4 cardamom pods
1 teaspoon black mustard seeds
1 teaspoon ajwain seeds
large bunch of coriander, big stalks
  removed, plus extra picked leaves to
  garnish
2 medium-hot green bullet chillies,
  deseeded and chopped
2 garlic cloves, peeled
olive oil, as needed
salt
splash of vegetable oil
4 x 175g cod fillets, lightly dusted
  with plain flour
knob of butter
ground ginger, to taste
freshly ground black pepper

Red Mullet with Vanilla Jerusalem Artichoke Purée and Roasted Stem Broccoli

The Jerusalem artichoke is related to the sunflower plant. It's amazing that such a massive plant produces such a small root vegetable, but what a flavour! Combining the sweet nuttiness of the vanilla with the silky, oily red mullet may seem strange, but wow, it's a sunflower on a plate.

1. Preheat the oven to 180°C/gas mark 4.

2. Heat a splash of rapeseed oil in a saucepan and sweat the artichokes over a gentle heat until softened. Add the butter and the seeds scraped from the vanilla pod along with the pod.

3. Cover with the stock and season to taste with salt and ginger. Cook gently over a medium heat for about 10 minutes until the artichokes are soft.

4. Remove the vanilla pod. Whizz the artichoke mixture with the cream in a blender, then pass through a sieve to create a smooth purée.

5. Line a baking tray with greaseproof paper. Rub the mullet fillets with 1 tablespoon rapeseed oil and place on the lined tray.

6. Blanch the broccoli in a saucepan of boiling salted water for about 2-3 minutes until just tender. Remove with a slotted spoon and pat dry.

7. Heat a little rapeseed oil in a large frying pan over a medium-high heat, add the broccoli and cook, turning frequently, for about 2 minutes until lightly browned. Season to taste with salt.

8. Meanwhile, put the fish in the oven for 5 minutes until just cooked through. Remove and season with a squeeze of lemon juice.

Spoon the artichoke purée onto serving plates and add the red mullet fillets. Dress the plate with the roasted broccoli, finished with a little vanilla-infused oil and garnish with chervil.

Serves 4

rapeseed oil, for cooking
8 Jerusalem artichokes, peeled and chopped
knob of salted butter
1 vanilla pod, split
600ml chicken stock
salt
ground ginger, to taste
50ml double cream
4 red mullet fillets, pin-boned (see page 79) and descaled if necessary (scrape the scales off using the back of a knife)
large bunch of stem broccoli
squeeze of lemon juice
vanilla-infused oil, to finish (light oil such as vegetable or rapeseed infused with vanilla seeds)
chervil, to garnish

Hoof
Horn
Snout
and Tail

Pastry chefs make cakes
Real chefs cook meat!

Peter J. Casson, aka Pete, Uncle Pete, Pee Wee or Mickey from EastEnders, is my pastry chef and, may I add, one of the best. When we first opened at Purnell's we had five chefs. I did meat, fish and the pass (aka the hot plate – the section of the kitchen that controls service, where the main dishes are plated). It was pretty brutal and lunches would be savage! I put this pork dish on the menu where I roasted the meat on the bone, as a whole rack. Before cooking, I would leave it out of the fridge under a wet cloth, to let it come to room temperature. It took about 40–50 minutes at a high temperature, so for lunch it went in the oven at 11.30am (I'd also have another on the side waiting). We were incredibly busy, getting smashed right in, sweating and running around. The timer went off, so I pulled the meat out, looked at it, and felt it with a chef-type touch. Why's that soft?, I wondered. I checked it again, looked at the timer, then looked at the oven, WTF?! Some bastard had turned my oven down. 'WHO THE FUCK…?' I shouted. By this time every chef had their head down, waiters had run for cover, I booted the oven door and shouted again.

'Errrr…It was me,' said Pee Wee, over on the pastry.
'What for?' I shouted back.
'Some biscuits, chef,' Pete replied.

At this point, I just got on with it and rode the back out of the unfortunate chef de partie on the garnish section, Dixon. Sounds sad, but when it goes wrong someone has to get it. It's like an unwritten law of the kitchen. By the time it was all back on track Pete was really sorry, Dixon was still crying and I had massive chest pains. I then spent the entire service explaining to Pete the science of cooking and resting meat, and the importance of residual heat! Pete continues to make extremely delicious biscuits, but he's also an expert in what we now call residual 'Pete'.

Chicken Cooked in Hay with Asparagus in Salted Butter and Asparagus Custard

Claude Bosi, my old head chef at Hibiscus, was the guy who really taught me how to be myself in a kitchen, to cook what I love and to believe in it, not just to follow others and trends. You can't go to bed thinking you're Alain Ducasse because you'll wake up and still be Glynn Purnell. It's so true, but there are things you can take and learn from. I cook my chicken in hay, which is quite classical. At Hibiscus we would cook guinea fowl with this sort of technique, using other things like pine or lavender. As far as I understand it, Claude's old head chef, the great Alan Passard, would cook chicken in a similar way, and this was passed on to Claude and then on to me. Each one of us would produce something slightly different and that's what is great about cooking. So for the garnish on the chicken, be daring and change it, use peas or beetroot instead of asparagus. Go on and mix it up because what's the worst that can happen? Go to bed yourself and wake up who you want to be.

1. Preheat the oven to 180°C/gas mark 4.

2. Heat a little olive oil in a flameproof casserole dish and brown the chicken on all sides. Remove from the dish and set aside.

3. Put the hay and thyme into the dish and then place the chicken on top. Pour 250ml of the stock over the contents of the dish. Place the lid on the dish and transfer to the oven for 25 minutes.

4. Pour the remainder of the stock into the dish and cook for a further 35 minutes, or until the chicken is cooked through. Lift the chicken out of the dish and leave to rest in a warm place.

5. Cook the asparagus stems in a large saucepan of boiling salted water for about 3 minutes, or until just tender. Add the spinach and bicarbonate of soda to the pan and cook for a further minute. Drain and then whizz in a blender to a smooth purée. Pour into a saucepan and keep warm.

6. Whisk the egg yolks and sugar together in a bowl and then add the warm purée. Transfer to a saucepan and cook over a medium heat until it thickens. Remove from the heat and season to taste with salt and ginger. Set aside.

7. Heat the butter in a saucepan and cook the rosemary and asparagus tips over a gentle heat for 3–5 minutes to allow the tips to soak up the butter.

Carve the chicken for four people and place on serving plates. Spoon the asparagus custard alongside the chicken and scatter the asparagus tips over the plate. Serve with new potatoes or a spring salad.

Serves 4

splash of olive oil
1 medium oven-ready chicken, about 1.5kg
3 large handfuls of pet shop hay
½ bunch of thyme
500ml hot chicken stock
20 asparagus spears, trimmed and stems and tips separated
salt
250g picked spinach
½ teaspoon bicarbonate of soda
3 large free-range egg yolks
10g caster sugar
ground ginger, to taste
150g salted butter
3 sprigs of rosemary
new potatoes or a spring salad, to serve

Chicken Thighs with Pea Custard and Pea Salad

Now the question is, are you a breast or a thigh man? If you're talking chicken, it has to be the thighs. They're the best part of the chicken and so tasty - the skin and the fat are fab. Here they're accompanied by a really good custard of pea, which is incredibly easy to make. The vanilla works well with the peas and the salty crisp chicken. The pea salad can be served cold or slightly warm, whichever you prefer, and you can add some buttered noodles or potatoes to the dish if want to carb it up, but remember - no carbs before marbs!

---

1. Preheat the oven to 180°C/gas mark 4.

2. Heat an ovenproof frying pan until hot, add a little vegetable oil and fry the chicken, skin side down, until the skin is golden brown. Transfer the pan to the oven and cook for a further 15 minutes, or until cooked through. Remove from the oven, season to taste with salt and leave to rest in a warm place.

3. Whisk together the egg yolks, sugar and seeds scraped from the vanilla pod in a bowl.

4. Blanch the frozen peas in salted water, then drain and whiz in a blender to a purée.

5. Warm the cream and puréed peas in a saucepan, then pour over the egg yolk mixture. Return the contents to the saucepan and whisk the mixture over a medium heat until it thickens to a custard consistency.

6. Pour into a bowl, cover closely with clingfilm to prevent a skin from forming and refrigerate.

7. Pulse the defrosted peas a couple of times in a blender. Add the fresh peas, shallot and marjoram. Season with curry powder, ginger and salt, then bring together with a little olive oil to create a pea salad.

Dress each serving plate with the pea custard, two chicken thighs and a generous spoonful of pea salad. Garnish with two or three pea shoots.

Serves 4

splash of vegetable oil
8 chicken thighs, boned but skin left on
salt
3 large free-range egg yolks
15g caster sugar
½ vanilla pod, split
25ml double cream
375g frozen peas
250g frozen peas, defrosted
100g fresh raw peas
1 shallot, peeled and diced
½ bunch of marjoram, leaves picked
pinch of curry powder
pinch of ground ginger
splash of olive oil
8-12 pea shoots, to garnish

Chicken Curry Pie

Football is one of my escapes. Down to the Blues I go, which is my beloved Birmingham City. It's a long, long road and we are a tough team to follow, mainly because we don't have much success! You can change your house, change your job, even change your wife. But you NEVER change your team. Anyway, back to food - this is my salute to the Balti pie from the football. I think if you make it, the success will be yours. KEEP RIGHT ON!

1. Put the lard, butter and water into a pan and heat until melted.

2. In a mixing bowl, combine the flour and salt. Add the beaten egg and beat, on a medium speed, using the paddle attachment on the food mixer for 1 minute.

3. Pour the melted lard and butter mixture into the bowl, increase the speed and beat the mixture for 2-3 minutes until fully combined and shiny.

4. Flatten out the mixture onto a lightly floured tray and refrigerate for 1 hour.

1. Preheat the oven to 200°C/gas mark 5.

2. Melt the butter in a pan and fry the shallot. Add the leek and garlic, then stir in the flour and spices and cook over a low heat.

3. Gradually add the stock, continually mixing over a low heat until the flour is cooked out and the mixture reaches a thick coating consistency.

4. Add the lemon juice and zest, and season with salt to taste. Add the coriander and mix. Remove from heat, allow to cool slightly, then add the chicken.

5. Remove the pastry from the fridge and roll out, on a floured surface, to a thickness of 5mm. Cut off ⅓ of the pastry and put to one side for the 'lid' of the pie. Use the larger piece to line a pie dish. Fill with the chicken mixture, cover with the remaining pastry and pinch/crimp around the edges to seal.

6. Brush the top of the pie with the egg wash and place into the oven. After 15 minutes, remove from the oven and brush with egg wash again. Reduce the oven temperature to 180°C/gas mark 4 and cook for a further 10 minutes. Allow to cool slightly before serving.

Serves 4

For the pastry
100g lard
100g butter
200ml water
500g plain flour
1½ tablespoon of salt
2 free-range eggs, beaten

For the filling
3 chicken breasts, roasted and cut
   into 2.5cm square pieces
100g butter
1 shallot, diced
1 leek, shredded
2 cloves garlic, crushed
100g plain flour
2 tablespoons mild curry powder
1 tablespoon freshly grated ginger
1 teaspoon ground cumin
1 teaspoon garam masala
500ml chicken stock
juice and zest of 1 lemon
½ bunch coriander
salt
1 free-range egg, beaten, to wash
   pastry

Pheasant 'Maryland'

Retro! Retro! Read all about it! This garnish is to cooking what flares and side burns are to fashion. When people see this recipe, they'll probably think I've lost the fucking plot, but it's proper sick! It works and it's great fun, and if you're up for deep-frying the banana with the skin on (make sure it's kept out of the fridge and is really dry), you'll get a delicious, rich, buttery banana.

Banana, sweetcorn fritters and lightly spiced, pot-roasted pheasant – it's a 70s classic from a 70s child. It's flares, it's disco and, best of all, it's delicious.

---

1. Preheat the oven to 170°C/gas mark 3.

2. Mix the paprika, Cajun spice mix and ginger together and rub the mixture all over the pheasants.

3. Heat a little vegetable oil in a flameproof casserole dish and brown the pheasants on all sides. Remove from dish and set aside.

4. Add the carrot, celery, onion and garlic to the dish and cook until lightly coloured, then return the pheasants to the dish.

5. Pour the brandy over the pheasants and set the alcohol alight, then add the stock. Put the lid on the dish and transfer to the oven for 12-15 minutes.

6. Lift the pheasants out of the dish and leave to rest in a warm place. Pour the liquor into a saucepan and simmer over a medium heat until reduced by half. Keep warm.

1. Put the flour in a bowl and make a well in the centre. Beat the egg with the beer and add to the well. Gradually beat the flour into the liquid to make a smooth batter, then stir in the sweetcorn, spring onions and chives. Season to taste with salt and ginger.

2. Heat the vegetable oil in a deep-fat fryer or deep saucepan until it reaches 180°C. Drop large spoonfuls of the fritter mixture into the hot oil and deep-fry for about 3 minutes until golden brown all over. Drain from the oil and keep warm.

Remove any moisture from the outside of the bananas and deep-fry in the fritter oil at 180°C for about 3 minutes until the skin is golden brown. Drain from the oil, pat dry and cut in half lengthways.

Remove the pheasant breast meat from the bone. Add the knob of butter and splash of cream to the sauce and stir well.

Place the meat on serving plates with a fritter and a piece of deep-fried banana. Drizzle with the sauce.

Serves 4

For the pheasant
1 teaspoon smoked paprika
1 teaspoon Cajun spice mix
1 teaspoon ground ginger
2 pheasants, crown only with
   wishbone removed
splash of vegetable oil
1 carrot, peeled and chopped
1 celery stick
1 onion, peeled and chopped
1 garlic clove, peeled
75ml brandy
200ml hot chicken stock
knob of butter
splash of double cream

For the sweetcorn fritters
100g self-raising flour
1 large free-range egg
3 tablespoons stout
195g can sweetcorn, drained
2 spring onions, thinly sliced
½ bunch of chives, chopped
salt
ground ginger, to taste
vegetable oil, for deep-frying

For the bananas
2 ripe bananas in their skins, at
   room temperature

Duck with Tamarind Jam, Liquorice Purée and Green Beans

Duck is a great meat, and tamarind is a fruit that goes well with both duck and foie gras, as it cuts through the fattiness. But the star of this dish is the liquorice. Although one of my favourite ingredients, it is a love-it-or-hate-it flavour. Maybe it's a hereditary thing because my dad loves it too. As a child he would always get a big box of it for Christmas (he still gets one now), and one year – I think he was around eight – after he had spent an excitable Christmas morning playing with his toys (which in those days was probably an orange and a handful of nuts) he ate his usual box of liquorice from his grandmother, who was a great cook – all in one go... the whole box! Then up the stairs to his bedroom he went and, on his big bouncy bed, started to jump up and down, and up and down, and up and down. He started to feel a churn and a grumble, and thinking it would be a little fart, he sharted. WOW! So the moral of this story is – don't eat a whole box of liquorice and then jump up and down in your PJs, as you may end up in the shit!
Try this dish. Liquorice tastes amazing (in moderation!) and, because of this story, always makes me smile.

---

1. Preheat the oven to 180°C/gas mark 4.

2. Put the tamarind into a saucepan with a splash of water and simmer for 15 minutes, or until softened. Pass through a sieve to make a paste, discarding the seeds.

3. Heat a little olive oil in a saucepan and sweat the shallot until soft but not coloured.

4. Add the tamarind paste to the shallot and mix together. Add the lime juice and soy sauce and cook for 1 minute. Remove from the heat, season to taste with salt and ginger and set aside.

5. Put the liquorice sweets into a separate saucepan and cover with the water. Cook over a medium heat until the sweets have melted and formed a smooth paste. Keep warm.

6. Blanch the green beans in a saucepan of boiling salted water for 2 minutes, then drain and refresh in iced water. Drain well again.

7. Place the duck breasts in an ovenproof frying pan, skin side down, and slowly bring up to a medium heat, draining the fat into a container as it cooks. After 7 minutes, transfer the pan to the oven and cook for a further 8-10 minutes. Remove the pan from the oven, turn the duck breasts over and lift out of the pan, then leave to rest in a warm place.

8. Throw the green beans into the frying pan and glaze with the juices. Add a splash of the reserved duck fat and a squeeze of lemon juice. Season with a little salt and ginger.

Arrange the green beans on serving plates. Carve each duck breast in two and then place two pieces on each plate on top of the green beans. Add a spoon of the tamarind jam and a dot of liquorice paste. Garnish with the wild rocket leaves.

Serves 4

15 fresh or dried tamarind pods, shelled
splash of olive oil
1 shallot, peeled and diced
juice of 1 lime
splash of dark soy sauce
salt
ground ginger, to taste
20 soft liquorice sweets (such as Pontefract Cakes)
150ml water
large bunch of fine green beans
4 duck breasts, skin lightly scored
squeeze of lemon juice
bunch of wild rocket, to garnish

Blue Steak with Egg and Salsify Chips

Steak and chips, DO NOT mess with it. It's an all-time classic, and with hollandaise sauce not to be beaten, true. But I have changed the chips to salsify and the sauce for a rich yolk, so I'm not trying to make it better than the classic, just trying a different move, like a dance move without the sequins. It's a cheeky little idea, tastes nice and will put a smile on your face, and I love making people smile. I bet if I was in a tight Lycra suit covered in sequins trying dance moves, that would make a few people smile! Blue steak mmmm, egg yolk mmmm, tight Lycra... not so sure. Enjoy.

1. Peel the salsify and cut into chip shapes. Blanch in a large saucepan of boiling salted water for 1 minute. Drain and transfer to a bowl of iced water to cool for a further minute, then drain and pat dry.

2. Heat a frying pan over a high heat. Brush the steak with some of the vegetable oil and season with salt and ground black pepper. When the pan is very hot, press the steak onto the pan and cook to seal it quickly on each side – 1–2 minutes per side should be enough.

3. Remove the steak from the pan and leave to rest in a warm place for about 5 minutes.

4. Mix the sea salt and crushed black pepper into the olive oil and leave to infuse.

5. Heat the remaining vegetable oil in the frying pan and fry the salsify chips over a medium heat for about 5 minutes until golden brown. Drain off the excess oil, if necessary, and season with sea salt.

6. Poach the egg yolk in a saucepan of barely simmering water for 1 minute. Remove with a slotted spoon and transfer to a folded piece of kitchen paper.

Carve the steak into slices and arrange on a serving plate. Season to taste with salt and ground black pepper and top with the poached egg yolk. Arrange the salsify chips around the side of the plate. Garnish with watercress, then finish with Parmesan shavings and a drizzle of the infused olive oil.

Serves 1

2 x 15cm salsify roots
salt
1 x 150g fillet steak
2 tablespoons vegetable oil
freshly ground black pepper
good pinch of coarse sea salt, plus
   extra for seasoning
good pinch of crushed black pepper
50ml olive oil
1 large free-range egg yolk
bunch of watercress, to garnish
Parmesan cheese shavings,
   to serve

Short Rib of Beef with Mussels, Parsley and Wild Garlic

Surf and turf – it's pretty old school, but there's nothing wrong with that. Old school always comes back round as a fusion or a trend, and for me it never goes away, the classic being fillet steak and lobster or oysters. I'm doing a beef and mussels recipe here that I like to think is a spring-cum-summer dish, as it's a lighter way of serving a slow-cooked piece of meat. The garlic and parsley really work with the salty 'sea-ness' of the mussels and make the dish come together, and the look of the whole thing is brilliant with the sticky brown beef and bright green sauce. Wow! Also, you get two dishes in one: if you want, cook the beef and serve with mash, then have the mussels in a bowl as a starter. It's fantastic.

1. Preheat the oven to 200°C/gas mark 6.

2. Heat a little vegetable oil in a roasting tin, or a flameproof casserole dish, over a high heat on the hob. When hot, add the short ribs and cook until browned and sealed on each side.

3. Add all the vegetables, herbs, garlic and crushed peppercorns to the roasting tin, then pour over the wine and stock.

4. Cover the roasting tin with foil and cook in the oven for 3 hours until the beef is tender.

5. Lift the beef out and leave to rest in a warm place. Pour the pan juices into a saucepan and simmer over a medium heat until reduced to a thick glaze. Set aside.

1. Heat a little butter in a large saucepan and sweat the shallots, garlic and parsley stalks over a gentle heat until softened.

2. Throw in the mussels and then add the cider and bring to the boil.

3. Cover with the lid to create steam and simmer for 3–4 minutes until all shells are open (discard any that remain closed). Strain off the cooking juices into a clean saucepan and set aside.

1. Whizz the parsley, garlic leaves and garlic clove in a blender to a pulp.

2. Beat the pulp into the softened butter.

3. Bring the mussel juices to a simmer, then whisk in the garlic and parsley butter and the cream until thick. Pass through a fine sieve. Add the mussels, in and out of the shells, to the sauce.

Place the meat on a plate and glaze with the juice reduction. Spoon the mussels in the sauce over the top and garnish with parsley leaves and borage flowers.

Serves 4

For the short rib
splash of vegetable oil
2 short ribs of beef, soaked in brine
  (see page 53) for 3 hours
1 carrot, peeled and chopped
1 onion, peeled and chopped
2 celery sticks, peeled and chopped
½ bunch of thyme, chopped
2 bay leaves, chopped
3 garlic cloves, peeled and crushed
10 black peppercorns, crushed
½ bottle (375ml) of red wine
375ml beef stock

For the mussels
knob of butter
2 shallots, peeled and chopped
1 garlic clove, peeled and crushed
3–4 parsley stalks
1.5kg live mussels, scrubbed and
  debearded
glass of dry cider

For the garlic and parsley sauce
½ bunch of flatleaf parsley, plus extra
  leaves to garnish
5–6 large wild garlic leaves
1 garlic clove, peeled and chopped
150g salted butter, softened
100ml double cream

To serve
borage flowers, to garnish

Roast Tail Fillet of Beef with Braised and Stuffed Celery and Celeriac Purée

Roast tail fillet of beef is a classy touch of cooking that's a bit more grown up than your usual roast beef. It's like a school blazer or a suit on an important day, not there to light the room up, but there to be counted; just a bit serious – and I can do serious. It has classic flavours with simple cooking techniques, so invite your boss round because this dish lets you show off but without the bells or whistles. I'd say it's on the edge of being boring, but still very, very tasty. If it was a sexual position, it'd be on top - like the missionary, and everyone loves that!

1. Preheat the oven to 200°C/gas mark 6.

2. Mix the celeriac, cream and water together in a saucepan over a gentle heat, then simmer, stirring occasionally, for 20 minutes until tender.

3. Whizz in a blender until smooth, season to taste with salt and ginger and set aside. Keep warm.

4. Place the tail fillets, bone side down, in a roasting tin and heat on the hob over a medium heat for 5 minutes.

5. Transfer the pan to the oven for 15 minutes, then remove from the heat and leave to rest in a warm place.

6. Heat a little vegetable oil in a small roasting tin on the hob and sweat the shallots over a gentle heat until soft, then stir in the garlic and thyme.

7. Add the Madeira, Marsala and ceps and simmer over a medium heat until the liquid has reduced by half.

8. Add the celery sticks and stir to coat in the mixture, then add the bay leaf and peppercorns. Pour in the stock, cover the roasting tin with foil and place in the oven for 15 minutes, or until the celery is tender.

9. Lift the celery out and set aside. Pass the juices through a sieve into a saucepan. Simmer over a medium heat until reduced by half, then stir in the red wine gravy.

10. Pulse the foie gras and bone marrow in a blender to a rough consistency. Mix in the chopped parsley. Fill the celery with the mixture.

11. Place the celery under a medium grill until the mixture melts.

Carve the beef and drizzle with the sauce. Serve with the stuffed celery, a generous helping of the celeriac purée and a parsley salad.

Serves 4

½ celeriac, peeled and chopped
300ml double cream
100ml water
salt
ground ginger, to taste
2 x 400-500g beef tail fillets,
  on the bone
splash of vegetable oil
2 shallots, peeled and chopped
1 garlic clove, peeled
3 sprigs of thyme
100ml Madeira
100ml Marsala
30g dried ceps
4 celery sticks (about 15cm long),
  peeled
1 bay leaf
6 black peppercorns
150ml hot beef stock
1 tablespoon Red Wine Gravy (see
  page 189)
30g foie gras
20g Smoked Bone Marrow (see
  page 18)
1 tablespoon chopped parsley
Parsley Salad, to serve (see page 119)

Glazed Pork Chops with Sauerkraut and Charcuterie Sauce

The sad, the lonely. The humble pork chop doesn't have the respect it deserves. It can be boring and disregarded as a lesser rock 'n' roll cut, but when cooked and treated well, it's a great, solid, flavoursome chunk of protein. And when it's served with one of the best sauces around – charcuterie sauce – it really sings out loud. I cooked something similar for the Roux Scholarship and it took me to the final. Sadly, I got smashed in on the big day; I think I left my balls at home. Anyway, it's a classic combo and the acidic smoky cabbage makes you sing in French with a German accent. So roll up your sleeves and tuck in with a large stein of beer, and you'll be umpapa-ing all night long.

1. Pre-heat the oven to 180°C/gas mark 4.

2. Heat the butter in a flameproof casserole dish on the hob and sweat the onion and garlic over a medium heat for about 3 minutes.

3. Add the bacon and cook for a further 5 minutes.

4. Add the cabbage, juniper berries, wine and water and cook for a further 5 minutes, or until it reaches a simmer.

5. Cover the casserole dish and place in the oven for 30 minutes.

6. Remove from the oven and keep warm.

1. Preheat the oven to 220°C/gas mark 7.

2. Heat the olive oil in an ovenproof frying pan and fry the pork chops with the rosemary and thyme sprigs and the trimmings from the chops on both sides for 1-2 minutes, or until golden brown all over. Transfer the pan to the oven and roast for 7-8 minutes, or until the pork is cooked through. Remove from the oven and leave the pork chops to rest in a warm place.

3. Return the pan to the heat and add the knob of butter and a squeeze of lemon juice. Stir in the shallots and cook for a few minutes. Add the vinegar and then simmer until reduced by two-thirds.

4. Add the cornichons and capers and the stock and simmer over a medium heat until the liquid is reduced by half.

5. Whisk in the remaining 70g butter and then add the cucumber. Stir in the mint and sage and set aside.

Place each chop on a serving plate with the sauerkraut. Pour the sauce over the meat, ensuring that the garnish is evenly distributed across the two plates.

Serves 2

For the sauerkraut
1 onion, peeled and shredded
1 clove of garlic, peeled and sliced
25g butter
5 slices of streaky bacon, cut into
   lardons
600g raw salted cabbage, washed –
   see note
1 teaspoon juniper berries
125ml white wine, preferably Alsace
150ml water

For the pork chops and charcuterie sauce
1 tablespoon olive oil
2 pork chops, trimmed (keep
   the leftovers)
sprig of rosemary
sprig of thyme
70g salted butter, plus an extra knob
thinly sliced zest and juice of
   ½ lemon
2 shallots, peeled and diced
3 tablespoons white wine vinegar
15g cornichons, diced
15g capers
300ml hot pork or chicken stock
30g cucumber, diced
10 mint leaves, finely shredded
6 sage leaves, finely shredded

Note
You can buy the cabbage already salted or you can salt your own: quarter a white cabbage, remove and discard the core and shred the leaves. Fill a large earthware dish with half the shredded cabbage and cover with a good handful of coarse rock salt. Add the remaining cabbage, cover with more salt, then cover with a plate that fits inside the dish. Leave the dish to salt in an cool place for three weeks. The cabbage will produce a liquid and its foam should be removed regularly. When no more foam is produced the cabbage is ready.

Roast Pork Belly with Shrimps, Apple and Capers

Pork belly is an amazing cut of meat. Where I am from, we call it belly draft. We would cut it into thin slices and slowly cook it under the grill till the fat started to spit out and flames would bellow out of the grill! The method in this recipe is a lot easier – and safer – and slow roasting it gives it a wonderful texture and flavour. All the juices are caught in the tray and that's when the fun starts, because you can make a beautiful rich sauce of apple, capers and sage, finished with sweet brown shrimps and crunchy gherkins, which is perfect with the soft pork. It's making my mouth water just thinking about it.

1. Preheat the oven to 190°C/gas mark 5.

2. Place the pork, skin side up, on a roasting rack in a roasting tin and stab all over with a roasting fork. Season all over with salt and black pepper.

3. Roast for about 2 hours, or until very tender. Remove from the oven and leave to rest in a warm place.

4. Add the shallot to the juices in the roasting tin and cook over a gentle heat on the hob until soft. Add the capers and apple juice and simmer until the mixture reduces to a sauce consistency.

5. Add the apple, shrimps, sage, parsley, cream and butter and stir well. Keep warm.

6. Place the pork, skin side up, under a hot grill to crisp the skin, watching carefully to prevent burning.

Carve the pork, then arrange the slices on serving plates. Spoon the shrimp stew all over the pork. Eat with a dollop of mash or crispy summer cabbage.

Serves 4

2kg piece of boneless pork belly
salt and freshly ground black pepper
½ shallot, peeled and finely diced
2 tablespoons baby capers
100ml apple juice
1 large English Bramley apple, peeled, cored and diced
500g raw shrimps, peeled and blanched
½ tablespoon chopped sage
1 tablespoon chopped flatleaf parsley
splash of double cream
knob of butter
mashed potatoes or summer cabbage, to serve

Lamb Baklava with Courgette Purée

Baklava is a pudding, but I'm not saying eat lamb for pudding, although being a massive meat eater myself I wouldn't have a problem with that. I've taken the pud and made it into a main dish. There's a little work involved, but it's worth the effort when you're done. Matched with the courgette it's a lovely combo, but parsnips would really work too, while varying the flavour of the honey can make a big difference to the end result, like lavender in summer or a deep natural honey in autumn. So this dish is for all seasons – just be brave and chop and change it as you like.

1. Preheat the oven to 180°C/gas mark 4.

2. Heat a little vegetable oil in a large flameproof casserole dish and sweat one of the onions, the carrot and the leek over a gentle heat until softened.

3. Add the lamb to the casserole dish along with the rosemary and thyme sprigs. Cover with water, place the lid on the dish, then transfer to the oven and cook for 2½ hours, or until the meat is very tender (almost falling apart).

4. Remove the casserole dish from the oven and leave to cool. While still warm, lift the lamb out of the dish and set aside. Pour the liquor into a saucepan and simmer until it begins to thicken – there should only be a small amount left. Squeeze the excess water from the gelatine, add to the pan and stir until dissolved. Set aside.

5. Pick the meat off the lamb bones and shred. Put into a bowl and add the honey, almonds, apricots, pistachios and the gelatine mixture. Season to taste with salt and add the cumin.

6. Line a baking tray with sides at least 3cm deep with clingfilm and spread the mixture out into an even layer about 2–3cm deep. Cover and leave in the fridge for at least 4 hours until set. Remove from the fridge and turn out of the tray, then cut into 8cm squares.

7. Beat the egg with a little water and brush onto a sheet of filo pastry. Place a square of the set lamb on the pastry and wrap in the pastry, ensuring that it is completely enclosed. Repeat with the remaining filo and lamb. Place the lamb parcels (baklava) on a baking tray and brush with the egg wash, then leave to rest.

8. Cut the courgettes in half lengthways, scoop out and discard the centre from each and then chop the remainder.

9. Heat a little vegetable oil in a sauté pan and sweat the remaining chopped onion and the garlic over a gentle heat until soft. Season to taste with salt.

10. Cook the courgettes in a saucepan of boiling water for about 5 minutes until tender. Drain, put into a blender with the onion and garlic and the cream and whizz until smooth. Pass through a sieve and set aside.

11. Bake the baklava for 10–12 minutes until brown. Remove from the oven and dust with icing sugar.

Spoon the courgette purée into the middle of each serving plate, then place the baklava on top. Serve with a green salad and soured cream.

Serves 4

vegetable oil, for sweating the vegetables
2 onions, peeled and chopped
1 carrot, peeled and chopped
1 leek, chopped
2 lamb shoulders, on the bone with the fat on
3 sprigs of rosemary
3 sprigs of thyme
8g gelatine leaves, soaked in cold water for 10 minutes
3 tablespoons lavender honey
100g flaked almonds
10 ready-to-eat dried apricots, finely diced
100g shelled pistachio nuts, chopped
salt
1 tablespoon ground cumin
1 large free-range egg
8 filo pastry sheets
3 medium courgettes
2 garlic cloves, peeled and chopped
splash of double cream
icing sugar, for dusting

To serve
green salad
soured cream

Roasted Spiced Lamb with Coconut Rice

I love spices, if you hadn't noticed by now. This spiced-up lamb dish is amazingly simply with the coconut rice. The idea is to drop this one slap bang in the middle of the table with the rice, lamb and a big bowl of salad. It's even better if you are cooking for guests – there's always one with too much to say who never shuts up, so give the fork and carving knife to them and get them to carve. See how loud they are then. Always get people involved with dinner.

1. Sit the lamb in a deep roasting tin and spread the masala spice mix all over. Drizzle with a bit of vegetable oil, then cover the tin with clingfilm and leave to marinate in the fridge for at least a couple of hours, ideally overnight.

2. Preheat the oven to 210°C/gas mark 6½.

3. Remove the lamb from the fridge 30 minutes before cooking and take off the clingfilm.

4. Roast the lamb for 15 minutes, then pour the water into the tin. Cover the tin with foil and cook for a further 40 minutes.

5. Drain the liquid off, then return the tin to the oven and cook for a further 30–35 minutes (for medium-rare meat; cook for 2 hours in total for well done).

6. 5 minutes before the end of the cooking time add the tomatoes, the sliced onions, coriander, lime juice, chillies and spring onions to the roasting tin with the lamb. Remove the lamb from the oven and leave to rest in a warm place before carving.

7. Wash and drain the rice. Melt 40g of the butter in a saucepan until foaming, then fry the chopped onion for 2–3 minutes, or until softened. Add the rice and stir until it is coated in the butter. Tip the rice and onion into a lidded ovenproof dish.

8. Bring the coconut milk and milk to the boil in a saucepan, then remove from the heat and pour over the rice. Stir well, then season with the salt.

9. Cover with a lid and bake in the oven for 12–15 minutes, or until the rice has absorbed all of the liquid and is al dente.

10. Cut up the remaining butter and dot over the rice, then re-cover and leave to melt for a few minutes before fluffing up the grains with a fork.

Carve the lamb into thick slices. Spoon the rice onto serving plates and spoon over some of the tomato and onion mixture from the roasting tin. Lay the slices of lamb over the rice, then add a spoonful of yogurt alongside and garnish with coriander shoots.

Serves 4

1.5kg leg of lamb (ask your butcher to remove the 'H' bone and thigh bone, leaving the shin bone in for presentation)
3 generous tablespoons Purnell's Masala Spice Mix (see page 194)
vegetable oil, for drizzling
250ml water
4 tomatoes, cut into eighths
2 small onions, peeled and sliced
½ bunch of coriander
squeeze of lime juice
2 green chillies, chopped
3 spring onions, chopped
200g basmati rice
70g butter
50g onion, peeled and finely chopped
400ml can full-fat coconut milk
200ml full-fat milk
pinch of salt
coriander shoots, to garnish
natural yogurt, to serve

Braised Elbow of Lamb (Shoulder Shanks) with Red Lentil Stew and Parsley Salad

Yes, I call this lamb elbow, and yes, I know sheep don't have elbows. As my old chum Sat Bains was saying, 'What's next, Chief? Ankle of lamb?' I did this dish live on TV. The night before filming I decided to catch up with some chef mates, which can sometimes be messy! Tom Kerridge, André Garrett, Sat Bains and I went off to MEATliquor – shots, burgers and beer. As expected, too much of a good time was had by all! Got back to the hotel at 4.30am and a car picked me and Sat up for filming at 6.20am. But, like true chef Spartans, we did it, and I'm sure the 2.5 million people watching had no idea we were hangin'. Anyway, lamb elbow with rich, wintery lentils and sharp parsley salad – it's mustard!

1. Preheat the oven to 200°C/gas mark 6.

2. Heat a little olive oil in a flameproof casserole dish and brown the lamb on all sides. Remove from the dish and set aside.

3. Add all the vegetables, the garlic and rosemary to the pan and cook until softened and golden brown. Add the ras-el-hanout and cook briefly, stirring, then stir in the red wine.

4. Return the lamb to the casserole and cover with the stock. Place the lid on the dish and transfer to the oven for 2½ hours. Check halfway through and add more stock if required.

5. When ready, lift the lamb out of the dish. Pass the stock through a sieve into a saucepan and simmer over a medium heat until reduced by half. Set aside.

1. Heat a little olive oil in a saucepan with and sweat the onion, garlic and carrot over a gentle heat until softened.

2. Add the lentils and then enough of the stock to half cover them. Simmer gently, adding more of the stock as it is absorbed, for about 20 minutes until the lentils are cooked and the consistency of a sauce, i.e. not too dry.

3. Season to taste with salt and cumin powder, and stir in the chopped parsley.

1. Put the shallot into a bowl and pour over the vinegar. Add the oil, anchovies and capers and mix together. Season to taste with salt.

2. Pour the dressing over the parsley and mix well.

Blowtorch the lamb until golden brown, or brush with a little oil and place under a hot grill. Transfer to serving plates, cover with the red lentil stew and serve with the parsley salad.

Serves 4

For the lamb
splash of vegetable oil
4 elbows of lamb (shoulder shanks)
1 onion, peeled and chopped
1 celery stick, chopped
1 carrot, peeled and chopped
3 garlic cloves, peeled and crushed
3 stalks of rosemary
1 tablespoon ras-el-hanout
glass of red wine
1.5 litres of hot lamb stock, plus extra
  if needed

For the red lentil stew
splash of vegetable oil
½ onion, peeled and diced
2 garlic cloves, peeled
½ carrot, peeled and diced
185g dried red lentils
reduced stock from braising lamb
  (see above)
salt and cumin powder
½ bunch of parsley, leaves picked and
  chopped

For the parsley salad
1 shallot, peeled and cut into rings
2 tablespoons white wine vinegar
100ml rapeseed oil
8 anchovy fillets
1 tablespoon capers
salt
small bunch of parsley, leaves picked

Roast Loin of Venison with Juniper Berries, Sweet and Sour Parsnips and Curly Kale

Game is not everyone's cup of tea, but early season venison is probably the easiest to eat, as it's not too strong. I don't eat venison out of season. It's the same as a strawberry - wait for it to come around once a year and enjoy it when it's at its best. Venison is really healthy for you too; not as fatty as beef or lamb, but still full of flavour. The loins are brilliant for this dish, but don't forget about the back legs, which are also great for stews and pies. The parsnips in this dish are amazing, though they're not so healthy. They're cooked in what we call a 'gastric', which is equal amounts of sugar and vinegar, to give them a sweet and sour flavour that cuts through the rich venison and marries well with the pear. Liquorice can also be a great addition to this dish, but that's up to you. So wait till the season starts in autumn and go out and cook venison. I promise, at the right time it's as good as beef.

---

1. Season the venison loins all over with black pepper and some of the ground juniper berries.

2. Roll each seasoned venison loin tightly in heatproof clingfilm to form four sausages.

3. Bring a saucepan of water to the boil, then reduce the heat until the water is simmering at roughly 65°C on a cooking thermometer. Add the wrapped venison loins, then return the water to 65°C and cook for 15 minutes.

4. Remove the poached venison loins from the water, unwrap and set aside.

5. Heat a frying pan over a medium to high heat until hot and then add half the butter. When the butter is foaming, add the venison and fry for 30-45 seconds on each side, or until just browned all over. Remove from the pan and leave to rest in a warm place for 5 minutes.

6. Bring the sugar and vinegar to the boil in a saucepan, add the remaining ground juniper berries and cook, stirring frequently, until the mixture is thick enough to coat the back of the spoon.

7. Add the parsnip ribbons, in batches if necessary, and boil for 5-10 minutes, or until tender. Remove from the poaching liquid, shake off any excess liquid and set aside. Keep warm.

8. Bring the stock to the boil in a separate saucepan, then reduce the heat to a simmer. Whisk in the remaining butter, then add the kale and cover the pan with the lid. Cook for 3-5 minutes, or until just tender, then season with salt and black pepper.

Carve each venison loin into three slices. Place three of the slices in a line down the centre of each serving plate. Top each piece of venison with some of the sweet and sour parsnip ribbons, then drizzle over the olive oil and season with salt. Spoon the kale alongside and spoon over the red wine gravy. Place the pear ribbons alongside each portion of venison if you like.

Serves 4

4 x 225g venison loins, fully trimmed
freshly ground black pepper
20 juniper berries, freshly ground
75g butter
110g caster sugar
110ml distilled malt vinegar
1 medium parsnip, peeled and sliced into ribbons on a mandolin
110ml chicken stock
200g kale, tough stalks removed
salt
1 tablespoon extra virgin olive oil
200ml Red Wine Gravy (see page 189), heated to boiling point
1 Conference pear, peeled, cored and halved, or sliced into ribbons lengthways on a mandolin, to serve (optional)

Faggots with Mushy Peas, Onion Gravy and Malt Vinegar and Black Pepper Glaze

Faggots are a really old dish using all the offal of the pig. What can be quite scary is the thought of a lung, heart and kidney staring at you - it's enough to make any meat eater a veggie! But faggots turn that scary stare into a delicious, rich, moist, sophisticated piece of cooking, and when matched with mushy peas and a sharp vinegar and black pepper glaze, it all comes together really well.

1. Drain the soaked peas, rinse under cold running water and drain again. Cover with fresh water, then drain again and put into a saucepan with the stock and bicarbonate of soda. Bring to the boil, skimming off any scum that rises to the surface.

2. Cook for about 30-40 minutes until the peas are soft. Drain and then season with salt and black pepper.

1. Preheat the oven to 180°C/gas mark 4.

2. Mix the chopped onions with the pig fry and pork belly in a casserole dish and add the water. Cover with the lid and cook in the oven for 45-50 minutes, or until the meat is tender. Leave to cool slightly, then strain off the liquor and reserve.

3. Pass all the cooked meat and onions through a meat mincer and put into a large bowl. Add the breadcrumbs, mace and sage, season with salt and black pepper and mix together well.

4. Using damp hands, roll the mixture into balls a little bigger than a golf ball, then wrap in the pork caul fat. Put into the casserole dish, add some of the reserved cooking liquor and cook in the oven, uncovered, for 10-15 minutes, or until the caul fat is golden brown.

5. Heat a little vegetable oil in a sauté pan with and sweat the thinly sliced onions over a gentle heat, covered, for about 3 minutes until soft but not coloured. Add the remaining cooking liquor and simmer, uncovered, until reduced to a sauce consistency. Season to taste with salt and black pepper.

Bring the ingredients to the boil in a small saucepan and then simmer over a medium heat for about 15 minutes until reduced to a thick syrup.

Brush each serving plate with the malt vinegar and black pepper glaze. Place two spoonfuls of mushy peas on each plate and top with two faggots. Spoon the onion gravy over the faggots.

Serves 4

For the mushy peas
300g dried split green peas, soaked in cold water overnight
700ml chicken stock
1 tablespoon bicarbonate of soda
salt and freshly ground black pepper

For the faggots and gravy
350g onions, peeled and half chopped, half thinly sliced
500g pig fry (liver and heart), cut into 4cm pieces
250g pork belly without skin, chopped
250ml water
75g fresh white breadcrumbs
pinch of ground mace
1 tablespoon chopped sage
salt and freshly ground black pepper
300g pork caul fat (available from some butchers)
splash of vegetable oil

For the malt vinegar and black pepper glaze
300g caster sugar
300ml distilled malt vinegar
1 tablespoon coarse ground black pepper

Shy
Babies
Get No Sweets

Ah,
the egg!

Burnt English Custard Egg Surprise has been on my menu since I won with it on the *Great British Menu* with a perfect score – 10, 10, 10. The presentation of this dish is not a new idea; it's been done for years. I saw it in France, and many other chefs have filled an eggshell with all sorts of things from savoury to sweet, soups to crèmes, chicken livers to scrambled eggs.

I won the dessert course on the show and the prize was to cook the dish as part of a banquet to be served to the world's most famous chefs, most of whom had three Michelin stars. If that wasn't enough to make my arse twitch, the GOD that is Heston Blumenthal, my hero, was going to be hosting. I think the tasting before service was more nerve-racking than the actual banquet, but Heston loved it – phew! The other two in the kitchen were Jason Atherton and Stephen Terry – two great chefs and very funny guys. We had a whale of a time. Jason and Stephen thought it would be clever to get me to make the tea. It backfired, though, when I used salt instead of sugar.

We were getting ready to start service and Heston turns up in the kitchen with ten of the world's best chefs, as you do. Getting to meet and chat to them was a real honour. Thomas Keller, the American multi-starred chef of The French Laundry and Per Se restaurants, came over to me along with Heston and asked, 'What are you cooking, chef?' I replied, 'The pudding, chef'. He then asked, 'Are you ready?', and I said, 'It's boxed'. He looked a little baffled and said, 'It's coming from a box?' Heston laughed and said, 'No chef, it is boxed'. The American chef looked even more bewildered, so Heston had to explain the Brummie expression. Once the penny dropped, he laughed and off they both went.

The banquet was a massive success and I enjoyed every minute of it. At the end of service there was one other chef I had to see, another GOD and hero of mine, Pierre Gagnaire. We got the opportunity to talk and I asked him what he thought not just of my food but also food fashions. He replied, 'To be the fashion is not to be the fashion'. We hugged and he kissed me, and our beards stuck like Velcro – a moment I will never forget!

Pineapple Upside Down Cake

Traditionally made with apples, cherries and other seasonal fruit, the famous upside down cake of old was cooked in a cast-iron skillet on top of the stove. Then, in 1925, Dole Pineapple (then called the Hawaiian Pineapple Company) asked people to submit recipe ideas using the fruit. They received 2,500 recipes for pineapple upside down cake. In this way not only was canned pineapple brought into the twentieth century, so was the famous upside down cake, which, when using pineapple, was oven-cooked, thereby creating the modern-day version.

1. Pour the pineapple juice into a medium saucepan and add the sugar, the seeds scraped from the vanilla pod along with the pod, the cinnamon stick, bay leaves and star anise. Bring the mixture to a simmer over a medium heat.

2. Skin and remove the eyes from the pineapple, then slice in half horizontally to create two round halves. Remove the core with an apple corer.

3. Place the pineapple in the pineapple liquor – it should be fully submerged. Poach the pineapple over a gentle heat for 45 minutes, or until a sharp knife goes through the surface of the pineapple with ease.

4. Remove the pan from the heat and leave the pineapple in the liquor, preferably for 24 hours, to allow the pineapple to take on the flavour of the liquor.

1. Whisk the yolks, eggs and sugar together in a large bowl until thick and pale.

2. Add the cream and cherry brandy to the mixture and whisk together.

3. Add 200g of the flour one-third at a time and mix until smooth. Pass the mixture through a sieve and then cover with clingfilm and refrigerate for 24 hours.

4. Before use, whisk in the remaining 100g flour until smooth.

1. Heat the sugar in a heavy-based saucepan over a medium heat until it starts to melt. Stir the sugar using a heatproof spatula to help evenly caramelise the sugar, ensuring that you stir right to the edge of the pan.

2. Once all the sugar has melted and you have a dark brown caramel, leave the mixture until it just starts to smoke and then remove from the heat. Add the water and whisk until you have a smooth caramel – you may need to put the pan over a medium heat to help with the mixing. When the water is added, the hot caramel will spit, so take care not to burn yourself during this process.

3. Pass the caramel through a sieve into a heatproof bowl and leave to cool slightly for 2–3 minutes. Slowly whisk in the butter, 1 tablespoon at a time. Once half the butter has been added, add the vanilla seeds and then the remaining butter. Set aside at room temperature until required. (The butterscotch will keep in the fridge for up to a month, but bring it up to room temperature before using.)

Serves 4

For the poached pineapple
1 litre pineapple juice
150g light soft brown sugar
1 vanilla pod, split
1 cinnamon stick
2 bay leaves
1 star anise
1 super-sweet pineapple

For the cake batter
6 large free-range egg yolks
3 whole free-range eggs
150g caster sugar
375ml double cream
75ml cherry brandy
300g strong white bread flour, sifted

For the butterscotch sauce
250g light soft brown sugar
50ml water
65g salted butter, softened
1 vanilla pod, split and the seeds scraped out

continued overleaf . . .

To assemble the cake

1. Preheat the oven to 180°C/gas mark 4.

2. For each cake, add 1 tablespoon of the butterscotch sauce to a 12cm blini pan.

3. Slice the pineapple into 1cm-thick slices. Place a pineapple ring in the pan and gently press down. Place the pan on a flat baking tray and put the tray into the oven. When the butterscotch starts to boil, remove the tray from the oven and, using tongs, carefully turn the pineapple ring over. Add a ladleful of the batter, just enough to cover the pineapple but not to reach the lip of the pan.

4. Return the tray to the oven and bake for 10–12 minutes, or until the top of the batter is dark brown. Remove the tray from the oven and turn the cake out of the pan onto the tray.

Put four or five dots of the butterscotch sauce on each serving plate. Place a cake on the plate and sprinkle five or six freeze-dried cherries per plate on and around the cake. Place a scoop of pineapple sorbet on top of each cake and serve immediately.

To serve
freeze-dried cherries
Pineapple Sorbet (see page 201)

Bakewell Tarts with Double Cream Ice Cream and Instant Fruit Jam

Bakewell is a small town in Derbyshire, a lovely little place, and this is where the cake comes from, hence the name. There are two types of tart in the town, each with its devotees who claim theirs to be the original, and there is a proper rivalry between the two fuelled by masses of passion – almost war! Sitting on the fence, I like them both, but try this one – it's delicious and the double cream ice cream will blow you away.

Serves 4

1. Mix the flour and sugar together in a bowl, add the butter and rub in with your fingertips until you have a crumb consistency.

2. Stir the egg into the mixture and then gently bring it together into a dough with your hands. The mixture should be a smooth yellow mass with no visible lumps of flour or butter.

3. Turn the pastry out onto a lightly floured surface and carefully flatten it until 1cm thick. Wrap the pastry in clingfilm and leave to rest in the fridge for a minimum of 2 hours (24 hours is preferable).

4. Take the pastry out of the fridge, unwrap and roll out on a lightly floured surface to about 4mm thick. Using a 12cm round pastry cutter, cut out four rounds and use to line four individual tartlet moulds or rings about 8-10cm in diameter. Alternatively, use the rolled-out pastry to line a 30cm flan ring to create one large tart.

5. Place the moulds/rings on a baking tray and leave to rest in the fridge for 2 hours.

6. Once the tartlet cases have rested, preheat the oven to 160°C/gas mark 3. Line the tartlet cases with heatproof clingfilm or baking parchment and fill with baking beans.

7. Blind bake the tartlet cases for 8-10 minutes, or until light brown. Do not allow the pastry to colour too much, or it will burn during the second cooking process. Remove from the oven and leave to cool for 10 minutes, then remove the clingfilm or parchment and baking beans.

For the sweet pastry cases
225g plain flour, plus extra for dusting
50g caster sugar
150g salted butter, diced
1 large free-range egg, lightly beaten

1. Gently mix the butter, sugar and almond essence together in a bowl and then, using a spatula, beat the mixture until it becomes pale and fluffy.

2. Add half the ground almonds and half the flour and mix together. Add the egg and continue to beat for 30 seconds. Add the remaining ground almonds and flour and beat the mixture until all the ingredients are fully incorporated.

3. Cover the bowl with clingfilm and set aside.

For the frangipane
50g salted butter
50g caster sugar
drop of almond essence
50g ground almonds
50g plain flour
1 large free-range egg
30g flaked almonds (untoasted)

continued overleaf ...

Bakewell Tarts with Double Cream Ice Cream and Instant Fruit Jam ctd

1. Bring the red fruit purée to the boil in a saucepan and mix in the brandy or cider brandy. Reserve 3 tablespoons of the purée for glazing the tarts.

2. Mix the sugar and pectin together in a separate bowl and then add to the fruit purée and whisk thoroughly.

3. Stir in all the berries and then remove the pan from the heat and leave the fruit mixture to cool in the pan.

4. Spoon into four small Kilner jars and set aside.

5. To heat the jam for serving, stand the jars in a deep baking tray and pour in boiling water to reach halfway up the jars.

1. Put the cream and milk into a saucepan and add the seeds scraped from the vanilla pod along with the pod. Bring the mixture to the boil.

2. Whisk the sugar and egg yolks together in a bowl until pale and fluffy, then pour the cream mixture over the eggs. Transfer the mixture to a saucepan and whisk over a low heat until the mixture is thick enough to coat the back of a spoon. Discard the vanilla pod.

3. Remove the pan from the heat and leave the mixture to cool. Churn in an ice-cream machine according to the manufacturer's instructions until almost set. Transfer to a freezerproof container and store in the freezer.

Glaze the tartlets with the reserved fruit purée and then fill them about two-thirds full with the frangipane. Sprinkle evenly with the flaked almonds and return to the oven for 8–10 minutes, or until the frangipane is golden brown.

Remove the tartlets from the oven, turn out of the moulds/rings and leave to cool slightly on a wire rack. Serve the tartlets warm, dusted with icing sugar. Add a scoop of the double cream ice cream and a jar of warm jam alongside.

For the hot fruit jam
100g red fruit purée
25ml brandy or 40ml cider brandy
25g caster sugar
3g pectin
30g blueberries
30g blackberries
30g hulled strawberries
30g raspberries

For the double cream ice cream
375ml double cream
125ml full-fat milk
1 vanilla pod, split
120g caster sugar
6 large free-range egg yolks

To serve
icing sugar, for dusting

Stuffed Baked Apple with Spiced Mascarpone

Stuffed apples, autumn, Christmas, winter – like the smell of a German market, like mulled wine; spicy, sweet and sharp. This dish comes out a little different every time, sometimes a little soggy, sometimes very sweet; it all depends on the apples. However it comes out, though, it's always a pleasure. It may not be the prettiest of puddings, but it packs a massive punch of flavour.

---

1. Preheat the oven to 160°C/gas mark 3.

2. Slice the tops off the apples and set the tops aside. Using a small spoon, remove and discard the core and flesh from each apple, leaving about 1cm of flesh remaining around the inside.

3. Squeeze the juice from the lemon half into a saucepan of boiling water, then add the lemon shell. Blanch the apples in the water for about 5 minutes until nearly cooked. Remove with a slotted spoon and plunge into iced water. When cool, remove and dry them off with kitchen paper.

4. Mix the mincemeat, prunes and apricots together in a bowl. Add the Calvados, lime zest and juice, cloves and basil.

5. Fill the apples with the mincemeat mixture and replace the tops.

6. Brush the filo pastry sheets with melted butter and then wrap each apple in pastry and dust with icing sugar.

7. Place the apples on a baking tray and bake for 10–15 minutes until golden brown. Remove from the oven and leave to cool slightly.

8. Beat together the mascarpone, cinnamon, ginger and the teaspoon of icing sugar in a bowl.

Place a spoonful of the spiced mascarpone onto each serving plate and arrange a warm apple alongside. Dust with icing sugar.

Serves 4

4 medium apples (Braeburn, Cox's or Pink Lady, according to the season)
½ lemon
100g mincemeat
12 prunes, soaked, pitted and diced
18 ready-to-eat dried apricots, diced
splash of Calvados
zest and juice of 1 lime
pinch of ground cloves
½ bunch of basil, finely shredded
8 sheets of filo pastry
30g butter, melted, for brushing the pastry
icing sugar, for dusting, plus an extra 1 teaspoon
200g mascarpone
pinch of ground cinnamon
pinch of ground ginger

Pavlova with Warm Cherries, Toasted Pistachios and Chantilly Cream

The big question is, what is in the middle of pavlova? Er... 'vlo' Funny? No, it's soft meringue with a hard shell. That's what this is if done properly. One tap of the spoon and 'BOOM', it smashes over warm cherries, caramelised nuts and sweet vanilla cream – DONE!

1. Preheat the oven to 130°C/gas mark ¾. Line a large baking tray with silicone or greaseproof paper.

2. Thoroughly mix 175g of the caster sugar and the cornflour together in a bowl.

3. Put the egg whites in an electric mixer fitted with a whisk attachment and whisk on full speed to volumise. Once doubled in volume, reduce the speed to medium and rain in the remaining caster sugar. Once all the sugar is added, return to full speed and then whisk for 2–3 minutes.

4. Add the malt vinegar and vanilla extract and whisk for 30 seconds.

5. While constantly whisking, rain in the sugar and cornflour mixture and mix for 1 minute.

6. Carefully spoon the mixture into a piping bag fitted with a medium round nozzle and pipe the mixture into ten 5–6cm-diameter domes with a 5cm gap between each one onto the lined baking tray.

7. Bake for 8 minutes, then turn the tray around and bake for a further 8 minutes.

8. Reduce the oven temperature to 110°C/gas mark ¼ and bake for a further 20–25 minutes. Remove one pavlova from the oven and leave to cool for 30 seconds. Break it in half and check that it's hard and crisp on the outside and light and fluffy on the inside.

9. Remove the remaining pavlovas from the oven and leave to cool on the baking tray.

1. Drain the kirsch from the cherries into a saucepan and bring to the boil over a medium heat.

2. Mix the sugar and pectin together, then whisk into the boiling kirsch. Reduce the heat and simmer for 5 minutes until thickened.

3. Add the cherries, stir and then remove the pan from the heat.

4. Pour the cherries and sauce into a bowl, lay clingfilm over the top and press down into the cherries to prevent a skin from forming. Set aside.

1. Lightly grease an A4-sized piece of silicone paper with sunflower oil and place on a baking tray.

2. Heat the teaspoon of sunflower oil in a non-stick frying pan and toast the pistachios until lightly coloured.

3. Stir in the icing sugar and cook until it has evenly caramelised around the nuts.

4. Add the butter and cook for a further 30 seconds, then turn out onto the silicone paper. Season with salt.

Serves 4

For the pavlova
525g caster sugar
1½ teaspoons cornflour
300ml free-range egg whites (about 10 egg whites)
1½ teaspoons distilled malt vinegar
1½ teaspoons vanilla extract

For the warm cherries
400g jar of Griottines (Morello cherries in Kirsch)
100g caster sugar
8g pectin

For the toasted pistachios
1 teaspoon sunflower oil, plus extra for greasing
100g shelled and skinned pistachio nuts
25g icing sugar, sifted
25g butter
salt

continued overleaf . . .

Combine the cream, sugar and seeds in a bowl and whisk until stiff peaks form. Cover and refrigerate until ready to serve.

Spoon a small amount of Chantilly cream in the centre of each serving bowl and place a pavlova on top. Warm the cherries gently and spoon around the pavlova with a little of the cherry kirsch sauce. Sprinkle over toasted pistachios and finish with a spoon of Chantilly cream.

For the Chantilly cream
200ml whipping cream
40g caster sugar
1 vanilla pod, split and seeds
 scraped out

Six-Inch String Trick

At 17 I was tall, thin and sported a fluff of a tash. A commis chef who thought he was God's gift to cooking. One morning, I was told to go to the butchers' unit to collect a meat order for the main kitchen. Often at this time some of the big boys would be there having a crafty coffee and reading the paper – usually a tabloid full of naked women and football. In any large kitchen there is always a 'clique', a gang of chefs who love a wind-up and run the kitchen a bit like the Mafia. Yes, a kitchen mafia. Being 17 and a commis left me vulnerable to pranks.

As I walked in to the butchers' unit, I was met by four or five chefs.
'Morning Glenda.'
'Morning Chefs. Can I have the meat?'
'Yeah, no problem.'
One guy then piped up with, 'Are you a betting man?'
I looked at him, looked around and realised that more chefs had squeezed their way in.
'Er, yes, I suppose so.' I replied nervously.
'Okay,' said the chef. 'I bet that I can tie you up with six inches of string.'
'No way!' I snapped back.
'Really?' he said, pulling a little piece of string out of his pocket and dangling it in front of my face. The atmosphere suddenly got a bit tense and it became deadly quiet.

The chef took the string, soaked it under the tap and then two of the other chefs grabbed my arms, put them behind my back and pushed my thumbs together. The chef then took the string and tied my thumbs. Now, with a large gathering of chefs behind me, I was marched out into the main kitchen and laid face down on the floor. They took my ankles, bent my legs back and tucked my feet underneath my tied thumbs. There were a few cheers and jeers and then they just carried on with their jobs, leaving me tied up like a piglet ready for the oven. The chefs were stepping over me, driving trolleys past me with huge smiles on their faces. Waitresses were laughing, as were the kitchen porters. After what felt like a lifetime, but was probably only about 10 minutes, my thumbs were full of blood and looked like two swollen cherry tomatoes! Eventually I was cut free and helped up.

I didn't take offence, as I realised it was just a bit of fun, but afterwards I walked with a bit less of a swagger. I later found out that one of the chefs had a brother in the army and that he was responsible for this Six-Inch String Trick.

Baked Vanilla and Blackberry Cheesecake

Cheesecake is a big favourite all over the world. There are good ones and really poor ones. This baked one is quality – I cooked it on the *Great British Food Revival*. People tend to overcook it, so my tip is to remove it from the oven when the cake still has a wibble, wobble. It will continue to cook outside the oven due to 'residual Pete'.

1. Pulse the digestives in a food processor into biscuit crumbs, then mix with the melted butter.

2. Press the biscuit crumb mixture into the base of a 23cm round cake tin, ensuring that the top is level. Chill in the fridge for 2 hours.

1. Put the berries and sugar into a saucepan with a splash of water and simmer over a gentle heat until the berries break down and become tender.

2. Whizz to a smooth purée in the food processor or a blender, then pass through a fine sieve into a bowl. Leave to cool.

1. Preheat the oven to 130°C/gas mark ¾.

2. Scrape the seeds from the vanilla pod into a bowl with the cream cheese and beat until well combined.

3. Whisk the eggs, lemon juice and cream together in a jug. Add half the egg mixture to the cream cheese and mix together until smooth and well combined.

4. Add the flour and sugar to the cream cheese mixture, then mix in the remaining egg mixture until smooth.

To assemble the cheesecake

1. Pour the cheesecake filling mixture onto the chilled crumb base and level, then drizzle over some of the blackberry purée.

2. Bake the cheesecake for 40 minutes, or until set but with a slight wobble in the middle and lightly golden on top. Set aside to cool and firm.

Cut the cheesecake into slices and serve with a little of the blackberry purée, fresh blackberries and a scoop of clotted cream.

Serves 6-8

For the cheesecake base
200g digestive biscuits
100g butter, melted

For the blackberry purée
125g fresh blackberries
2 teaspoons caster sugar

For the cheesecake filling
1 vanilla pod, split and seeds
   scraped out
500g full-fat cream cheese
3 large free-range eggs
juice of ½ lemon
75ml double cream
60g plain flour
200g caster sugar

To serve
punnet of fresh blackberries
250g clotted cream

Lemon and Lime Posset with Tamarillo and Basil Jam

Lemon posset is the perfect Sunday lunch pud and can be made well in advance. It is so easy too - it was one of the first puddings I made. In fact, it's child's play really, and there is hardly any washing up, which is music to everyone's ears. Adding lime makes it very special, and the tamarillo and basil jam gives it a facelift. The jam can also be used with pork or turkey.
#justsaying

1. Bring the cream and sugar to the boil in a saucepan. Reduce the heat and simmer for 3-5 minutes to reduce the mixture slightly.

2. Add the lemon and lime zest and juice to the mixture and simmer for a further 2 minutes.

3. Pour evenly into four glasses and chill in the fridge for about 2 hours until set.

1. Heat the tamarillos in a saucepan, add the sugar and cook over a gentle heat for 10 minutes, or until a thick, jam-like consistency.

2. Add the lime zest and juice and vanilla pod and cook until the mixture thickens. Remove the vanilla pod and leave to cool completely.

3. Before serving, add the chopped basil and a twist of black pepper.

Take the posset out of the fridge at least 30 minutes before serving. Add a tablespoon of jam to the each and decorate with small basil leaves. Dust with icing sugar.

Serves 4

For the posset
900ml double cream
250g caster sugar
zest and juice of 1½ lemons
zest and juice of 1½ limes

For the jam
4 tamarillos, peeled and chopped
100g caster sugar
zest and juice of 1 lime
1 vanilla pod, split
½ bunch of basil, leaves picked and
  finely chopped
freshly ground black pepper

To serve
small basil leaves, or a spring, to
  decorate
icing sugar, for dusting

Cassis Pâte de Fruits

These are like posh Haribo with no gelatine. It's all about cooking the sugar to the correct density. At Purnell's we serve them with our peanut butter lollipops (see page 160) to go with your coffee. I saw these when I was working in Lyon in France in a one-star restaurant. I put star anise in them to add aromatic flavour and citric acid in the sugar for a sour taste – not too much, though, otherwise your arse will bite your shoulder.

1. Lightly grease a 15cm square baking tray (or a casserole dish at least 2.5cm deep) with olive oil and then line with clingfilm.

2. Bring the blackcurrant purée and star anise to the boil in a large, heavy-based saucepan over a medium heat. Stir with a wooden spoon or heatproof spatula and then leave to boil for 1 minute.

3. Put 100g of the caster sugar into a bowl and mix in the pectin. Whisk into the blackcurrant purée and boil for 2 minutes, or until a skin has formed. (Keep the whisk and spoon or spatula in a jug of warm water to keep clean.)

4. Add another 250g of the caster sugar to the pan and whisk, then leave to boil for 2 minutes. Add the glucose and fondant icing sugar and whisk thoroughly. Clean down the sides of the pan using the spoon or spatula.

5. Place a sugar thermometer in the saucepan and boil without stirring until the mixture reaches 110°C.

6. Pass the mixture through a sieve into the lined baking tray. Gently tap the tray to level the mixture and then place on a wire rack. Leave to cool and set for 2 hours at room temperature, uncovered.

7. Mix the remaining caster sugar with the citric acid and put into an airtight container.

8. Turn the set blackcurrant mixture out from the lined tray and use a serrated knife, dipped in hot water and then dried, to cut into cubes.

9. Store the cubes in an airtight container lined with baking parchment paper in the fridge. They will keep for 3-4 weeks.

Before serving, roll the pâte de fruit cubes in the citric sugar mix.

Makes 50-60

olive oil, for greasing
500g blackcurrant purée
2 star anise
500g caster sugar
12g pectin
150ml liquid glucose
125g fondant icing sugar
15g citric acid

Marshmallow

Marshmallow comes from a plant, or at least it used to at one time, unlike the ones you buy now. But I can quite easily smash a big bag of those down - they're my favourites. As a kid we would call them flumps; don't know why, but we did. They're an easy little sweet to make, so go on and treat yourself to big clouds of sweetness - what could be better? Toast them, dunk them into hot chocolate and have fun, fun, fun! My tip is to put a little brandy in the hot chocolate!

1. Lightly grease a baking tray, about 25 x 30cm, with sides 7cm deep, with olive oil and then line with clingfilm.

2. Put the egg whites and vanilla seeds or vanilla extract into an electric mixer fitted with a whisk attachment.

3. Squeeze the excess water from the soaked gelatine and put into a small saucepan. Add the water and heat gently, stirring, until the gelatine has melted. Remove from the heat and set aside in a warm place.

4. Put the sugar into a heavy-based saucepan and add enough cold water to just cover the sugar. Heat over a medium heat until the sugar has dissolved. Place a sugar thermometer in the pan. Increase the heat slightly and bring to the boil. Every now and then, brush the sides of the pan with a pastry brush dipped in cold water to prevent sugar crystals forming.

5. Now start to whisk the egg whites with the mixer on a medium speed until they double in volume.

6. Once the sugar reaches 121°C, remove the thermometer and pour the sugar solution slowly and carefully onto the egg whites. Avoid pouring the syrup directly onto the whisk attachment. Continue to whisk until the mixture is cool.

7. Once cool, reduce the mixer speed to low and pour in the melted gelatine. Mix for 30 seconds. Using a spatula, scoop out the marshmallow mixture into the lined tray and spread using a crank-handled palette knife for a smooth finish - do this quickly, as the mixture will begin to set. Allow to cool slightly, then cover with clingfilm and refrigerate for 2 hours.

8. Dust a chopping board with cornflour and turn the marshmallow out onto the board. Dust the marshmallow with cornflour. Dip a knife into hot water and then dry it. Use the hot knife to cut the marshmallow into 3cm-wide strips and then cut the strips into squares.

9. Place in an airtight container and store in the fridge. The marshmallows will keep for up to 1 week.

Makes about 80

olive oil, for greasing
3 large free-range egg whites
1 vanilla pod, split and seeds scraped out, or 1 teaspoon vanilla extract
24g gelatine leaves, soaked in cold water for 10 minutes
1 tablespoon water
225g caster sugar
cornflour, for dusting

Lemon Verbena Panna Cotta with Poached Rhubarb, Rhubarb Sorbet and Sweet Toasted Seeds

Lemon verbena - what a great ingredient. Although very underused, it gives a lovely aromatic lemon flavour that's both unusual yet strangely familiar. But it does look a bit odd, like a massive pre-historic plant.
Rhubarb and lemon flavours, crunchy seeds, soft cream - this pudding has the lot. At Purnell's we serve it in Kilner jars, which looks the dog's!

1. Bring the cream and lemon verbena to a rolling boil in a large saucepan for 2 minutes, then reduce the heat and simmer for 5 minutes. Remove from the heat and leave to infuse.

2. Heat the milk and sugar in a medium saucepan until the sugar has dissolved.

3. Squeeze the excess water from the gelatine and stir it into the milk mixture until dissolved. Add the milk mixture to the infused cream and gently whisk. Pass the mixture through a fine sieve into a large pouring jug. Cover the top of the jug with clingfilm and push it down so that it is touching the mixture - this will prevent a skin from forming. Refrigerate for about 20 minutes until cool but do not allow to set.

4. Pour the cooled mixture, about 3cm deep, into four bowls about 12cm in diameter or 700ml/7cm-diameter Kilner jars and refrigerate until the mixture has set.

1. Put the cranberry juice, stock syrup and vanilla pod into a wide saucepan over a medium heat and bring up to a gentle simmer.

2. Gently add the rhubarb batons - they should be completely covered; if not, add more cranberry juice as required. Poach the rhubarb for 5 minutes, or until a sharp knife can push through it with little resistance.

3. Carefully lift out the rhubarb and set aside, then leave the liquor to cool.

4. Once cooled, the rhubarb can be stored in the liquor for up to 1 week.

Serves 4

For the panna cotta
500ml double cream
15g lemon verbena
150ml full-fat milk
110g caster sugar
6g gelatine leaves, soaked in cold
   water for 10 minutes

For the poached rhubarb
200ml cranberry juice, plus extra
   if needed
200ml Stock Syrup (see page 198)
1 vanilla pod, split
8 rhubarb stalks, cut into 7.5cm batons

continued overleaf

Lemon Verbena Panna Cotta with Poached Rhubarb, Rhubarb Sorbet and Sweet Toasted Seeds ctd

1. Preheat the oven to 150°C/gas mark 2 and line a baking tray about 7.5cm deep with silicone or greaseproof paper.

2. Mix together the oats, all the seeds, wheatgerm and sugar thoroughly with your hands in a large bowl.

3. Add the honey and oil to the bowl and mix again with your hands, ensuring that the dry ingredients are evenly coated.

4. Spread the seed mixture onto the tray. Bake for 15-25 minutes until golden brown, stirring every 5 minutes so that the seeds are evenly toasted. Remove from the oven and leave to cool in the tray.

Remove the bowls from the fridge and evenly sprinkle 2 tablespoons of the toasted seeds onto the panna cotta. Place three batons of poached rhubarb in the centre of each bowl and top with a scoop of rhubarb sorbet.

For the sweet toasted seeds
350g jumbo porridge oats
100g sunflower seeds
100g pumpkin seeds
50g black sesame seeds
50g white sesame seeds
50g blue poppy seeds
100g wheatgerm
75g demerara sugar
100g runny honey
75ml olive oil

To serve
Rhubarb Sorbet (see page 198)

Chocolate and Passion Fruit Domes

These look amazing, and although you might think it's a restaurant dish, it really can be done at home too. Chocolate with passion fruit is always a winner - the sharpness of the fruit really works with the bitterness of the chocolate, and it is perfect to follow a rich main course.

1. Heat the passion fruit and mango in a saucepan over a gentle heat until the fruit starts to break down.

2. Add the orange juice and sugar and continue to cook until the fruit has completely broken down.

3. Whizz the fruit mixture in a blender and then pass through a fine sieve. The mixture should coat the back of a spoon; if not, return to the pan and heat until a coating consistency is achieved.

1. Break the chocolate into pieces and put into a glass bowl set over a saucepan of hot water over a medium heat, ensuring that the water doesn't touch the base of the bowl. Leave until the chocolate is completely melted.

2. Remove the pan from the heat and stir the sunflower oil into the melted chocolate. Leave the bowl resting on the pan.

3. In a separate bowl, gently whip the cream until soft peaks form. Fold in the passion fruit purée.

4. Remove the glass bowl from the pan and carefully dry the base of the bowl. While constantly folding the cream mixture, pour the melted chocolate into the cream mixture - this must be done quickly to prevent the chocolate from setting, as this will cause the mixture to become grainy.

5. Once the mixture is fully combined, spoon it into a piping bag fitted with a medium round nozzle and then pipe the mixture into ten 6cm dome-shaped moulds. Use a palette knife to smooth the base of the domes and then place the moulds in the freezer for 24 hours.

6. Once the domes are fully frozen, line a flat tray with silicone or greaseproof paper and turn the domes out of the moulds onto the tray. Cover with clingfilm and place the tray in the freezer.

7. Melt the 300g dark or milk chocolate as in step 1, then remove from the heat and leave to cool slightly.

8. Remove the domes from the freezer. Carefully push a cocktail stick halfway into a dome and use the stick to dip the dome into the melted chocolate. Ensure that the whole of the dome is covered in chocolate and then gently shake it from side to side to remove the excess.

9. Carefully place the dome back onto the tray and gently twist the cocktail stick to remove it. Dip the stick into the melted chocolate and use it fill in the hole left by the stick.

Serves 4

For the passion fruit purée
3 passion fruit, halved and flesh and seeds scooped out
½ large mango, stoned, peeled and chopped
100ml fresh orange juice
1 tablespoon icing sugar

For the domes
450g dark chocolate (72% cocoa solids), plus an extra 300g (or milk chocolate, 42% cocoa solids) for coating
15ml sunflower oil
900ml double cream
200g passion fruit purée (see above)
50g dark, milk or white chocolate, to decorate

continued overleaf

Chocolate and Passion Fruit Domes ctd

10. Repeat the dipping process with all the domes, then place a sheet of silicone or greaseproof paper over them to cover the size of the tray. Cover entirely with clingfilm and then place the tray in the fridge.

11. Melt the dark, milk or white chocolate for decorating as in step 1, then remove from the heat. Remove the domes from the fridge, uncover and decorate them using a fork dipped into the melted chocolate to create a striped effect.

Once decorated, place the domes in the fridge for 3 hours before serving. This will prevent the outer chocolate from melting, while allowing the frozen centre to defrost.

Lemon Shortbread

Shortbread is 'dirk', which means great, mustard, brilliant! It's soo crumbly and short. This is a lovely little recipe and you can add black pepper if you want to try something different or do it as it is. Either way you will love it. We serve this with our Pauper's Cake (see page 154) at the restaurant. It's pretty easy to do, so give it a go.

1. Put the flour and butter into an electric mixer fitted with a paddle attachment and mix on a medium speed until you have a crumb consistency.

2. Add the icing sugar, lemon zest and salt and continue to mix on a medium speed for 2 minutes.

3. Add the vanilla extract and lemon juice and mix for a further minute.

4. Add the egg yolks and mix for 10-15 seconds only.

5. Turn out the mixture onto a lightly floured surface, using a spatula to scrape the bowl to remove all the mixture. Continue to mix with your hands – this will ensure that the pastry is light and crumbly in texture.

6. Divide the mixture into four, shape each into a ball and gently flatten. Cover with clingfilm and leave to rest in the fridge for 2-3 hours.

7. When ready to bake, preheat the oven to 150°C/gas mark 2.

8. Remove the shortbread mixture from the fridge and uncover. Lightly flour a clean, dry surface and roll out each portion evenly into a round about 8-10mm thick.

9. Line a baking tray with silicone or greaseproof paper and then place the pastry rounds on the tray - roll them around the rolling pin to transfer if necessary.

10. Bake for 15-20 minutes, or until the shortbread just starts to colour.

Remove from the oven, grate lemon zest over the top and sprinkle with caster sugar. Leave to cool on the baking tray before serving.

Serves 4

250g plain flour, plus extra for dusting
200g salted butter, diced
100g icing sugar, sifted
zest and juice of 1 lemon, plus extra
  zest to decorate
2g table salt
1 teaspoon vanilla extract
2 large free-range egg yolks
caster sugar, for sprinkling

Mince Pie Roll

It's beginning to look a lot like Christmas!
I make this every year with my kids. We have great fun and it makes the house smell lovely and festive. Give it a go if you want Christmas all around you - believe me, the ingredients end up all over your kitchen if your little ones are anything like mine.

1. Preheat the oven to 200°C/gas mark 6.

2. Mix together the mincemeat, cherries, apricots and lime zest and juice in a bowl, then stir in the basil leaves and allspice.

3. Lay the pastry on a lightly floured surface with a short edge nearest to you. Spoon the mincemeat mixture onto the pastry and form into a sausage shape across the width of the pastry partway down the length, as you would for a big sausage roll. Brush the edges of the pastry with egg wash along the nearest short edge of the pastry and along the other side of the mincemeat to aid sticking. Roll the pastry up around the mincemeat filling and trim off the excess.

4. Brush the roll all over with egg wash. Use scissors to snip and pinch the pastry at regular intervals along the roll to create a decorative effect. Sprinkle with sugar.

5. Transfer the roll to a baking tray and bake for 15-20 minutes until the pastry is golden brown and the filling is cooked through.

Leave to rest for 10 minutes, then slice and enjoy or tear and share.

Serves 4-6

450g jar of mincemeat
150g Griottines (Morello cherries in Kirsch), drained
150g ready-to-eat dried apricots, diced
zest of 1 lime and juice of ½
4 shredded basil leaves
pinch of ground allspice
1 sheet of all-butter puff pastry, rolled ½cm thick, 38 x 10cm
plain flour, for dusting
1 large free-range egg, beaten with a splash of double cream
granulated sugar, for sprinkling

Warm Chocolate Mousse with Chocolate Crumble, Tuile and Mint Ice Cream

Mint and chocolate is a classic combo – I love it. It would be an argument to the death with my brother and sisters about which was the coldest ice cream – mint chocolate chip of course! True, but then again not; it's actually the menthol in the mint that creates the extra cooling effect.

This dish is complex, but broken down you can then use the individual elements in different dishes – the crumble, the foam, the ice cream. Or you can really go for it and create the whole dish. It's a show-stopper.

1. Break the chocolate into pieces and put into a large bowl.

2. Bring the cream to the boil in a saucepan, then pour over the chocolate and stir until the chocolate melts.

3. Add the egg whites to the mixture and whisk until emulsified.

4. Pour into an espuma gun and charge with gas according to the manufacturer's instructions. Keep in a saucepan of warm water until ready to serve.

1. Preheat the oven to 180°C/gas mark 4.

2. Mix the flour, cocoa powder and sugar together in a large bowl, add the butter and rub in with your fingertips until you have a crumb consistency.

3. Line a baking tray with silicone or greaseproof paper, spread out the crumb mixture on the tray and bake, turning every couple of minutes, for 10–15 minutes until crumbly. Remove from the oven and leave to cool.

1. Preheat the oven to 160°C/gas mark 3.

2. Bring the sugar, butter, glucose and milk to the boil in a saucepan, then whisk in the cocoa powder until well combined.

3. Line a baking tray with silicone or greaseproof paper and spread the mixture thinly on the tray. Bake for 10–12 minutes.

4. Remove from the oven and leave it to cool and harden.

1. Mix all the ingredients together in a large saucepan and gently heat the mixture until it reaches 82°C on a cooking thermometer.

2. Remove from the heat and pass through a fine sieve into a bowl, then leave to cool.

3. Churn in an ice-cream machine according to the manufacturer's instructions until almost set. Transfer to a freezerproof container and store in the freezer until ready to serve.

Serve in medium-sized bowls. Line the base of each bowl with chocolate crumble. Break the tuile into small shards and scatter over the crumble. Place a scoop of mint ice cream on top and then jet the warm mousse over the ice cream to cover the contents of the bowl. Sprinkle the chocolate crumble on top.

Serves 4

For the chocolate mousse
200g dark chocolate (70% cocoa solids)
150ml double cream
150ml free-range egg whites (about 5 egg whites)

For the chocolate crumble
210g plain flour
15g cocoa powder
60g caster sugar
110g butter, diced

For the chocolate tuile
100g caster sugar
85g butter
35g glucose syrup
35ml full-fat milk
10g cocoa powder

For the mint ice cream
500ml single cream
100g caster sugar
65ml crème de menthe verte
50ml inverted sugar syrup
4g xanthan gum (available from health-food shops and online)
5ml mint essence
5 drops of green food colour

Pauper's Cake

One of the earliest recorded treacle tart recipes dates back to 1889. It was around this time that some of society's poorest people started to buy 'treacle' because it was regarded as an unwanted by-product of the pure white refined granulated sugar, which is what the affluent and rich would have in their kitchens. The discarded 'treacle' was sold for a pittance, almost given away. So poorer families, when any remaining bread became stale, would break the bread up into small pieces and mix it with the warm treacle in a large skillet pan and add a few spices like ginger or whatever was in their larder. They would leave the skillet pan over an open fire until it cooked and set. They would then eat large spoonfuls with homemade dairy produce from their own cows. This ensured that no food went to waste. This is our version of the early treacle tart in honour of the paupers, hence the name.

Luke Butcher, Pastry Chef at Purnell's

1. Preheat the oven to 160°C/gas mark 3.

2. Grease a 25 x 20cm cake tin with a little butter and line with silicone or greaseproof paper.

3. Bring the golden syrup, cream and butter to the boil in a saucepan, stirring occasionally. Remove from the heat.

4. Gently whisk the breadcrumbs, orange and lemon zest and salt together in a bowl. Add the syrup mixture and whisk gently until well combined.

5. Add the orange and lemon juice to the mixture and whisk together.

6. Crack the eggs into a separate bowl, ensuring that there is no shell in the bowl. Add the eggs to the mixture and whisk together until fully incorporated.

7. Pour the mixture into the prepared cake tin and use a spatula to ensure that all the mixture is removed from the bowl. Carefully smooth off the top of the mixture and then bake for 15-20 minutes. If it appears to be cooking too quickly, reduce the cooking temperature by 10°C.

8. Remove from the oven and carefully push a metal skewer into the centre. If it comes out clean, it's ready; if not, return to the oven for 2-3 minutes, or until the skewer comes out clean.

9. Place the cake tin on a wire rack to cool slightly.

While still warm, turn the cake out of the tin, cut into 2 x 5cm rectangular pieces and place a piece on each serving plate. Sprinkle with broken shards of lemon shortbread, add a quenelle (see page 39) of apple sorbet and decorate with candied zest.

Makes a 25 x 20cm cake

400g golden syrup
100ml double cream
75g salted butter, plus extra for greasing
275g fresh white breadcrumbs
zest and juice of 1 orange
zest and juice of 1 lemon
3g table salt
2 large free-range eggs

To serve
Lemon Shortbread (see page 150)
Apple Sorbet (see page 201)
Candied Zest (see page 202)

Chocolate Brownies with Peaches Cooked in Muscovado and Cava

Cava? Really? It is a lot cheaper than Champagne and I first used it when I worked in Vitoria in northern Spain. What an amazing place. The food, the landscape and the people. The food, from the fine fare of the starred restaurants down to the pinchos (a Basque word for tapas), was mind blowing. I had a great time and loved the way they used their local produce. The whole Rioja region is buzzing with culinary delights. The warm peaches and hot chocolate make this a proper pud, whether in Spain or Birmingham.

1. Beat the melted chocolate and butter together in a bowl.

2. In a separate bowl, mix together the icing sugar, eggs, flour, yeast, salt and all the nuts.

3. Lightly grease a 25 x 15cm baking tray, about 3cm deep, with sunflower oil and then line with clingfilm.

4. Mix the two mixtures together and then pour into the lined tray. Cover with clingfilm and place in the freezer for at least 3 hours until frozen.

5. Preheat the oven to 200°C/gas mark 6.

6. Remove the brownie tray from the freezer, uncover and cut the brownie into 5cm blocks or 4cm rounds.

7. Place the brownies on a baking tray and bake in the oven for 6–8 minutes. Leave to cool slightly on the tray.

1. Heat a saucepan with a knob of butter over a medium heat, add the peaches and cook for about 3 minutes until coloured.

2. Remove the peaches from the pan and then add the sugar and cook for about 2 minutes until caramelised. Add the cava and mix thoroughly.

3. Return the peaches to the pan and add the remaining 70g butter and the thyme sprigs. Mix thoroughly and then finish with a squeeze of lime juice.

Place a warm brownie on each serving plate and spoon the peaches around the brownie. Drizzle the peach juices over the top of the brownie and sprinkle with a little rock salt. Add a scoop of vanilla ice cream and decorate with thyme flowers, if available.

Serves 4

For the chocolate brownie
270g 72% dark chocolate, melted (see page 147), preferably Valrhona
160g salted butter, softened
330g icing sugar, sifted
4 large free-range eggs
260g plain flour
10g fresh yeast, crumbled
3g salt
50g walnuts, chopped
50g shelled pistachio nuts, chopped
50g blanched almonds, chopped
sunflower oil, for greasing

For the peaches
70g salted butter, plus an extra knob
3 large peaches, halved, stoned and then halved again
200g dark muscovado sugar
400ml cava
4 large sprigs of thyme (retain flowers to decorate, if available)
squeeze of lime juice

To serve
rock salt, for sprinkling
Vanilla Ice Cream (see page 202)

White Chocolate and Coconut Ganache

White chocolate mice and these little fellas in a paper bag is what I would call a mix-up – 'A ten pence mix-up, please', I would ask the shopkeeper. You can't buy anything for that these days. God I sound old! Well, this is my homage to the mix-up to the value of ten pence from all those years ago. The rainbow sprinkles are very important to bring back the memories.

1. Break the chocolate into pieces and put into a glass bowl set over a saucepan of hot water over a medium heat, ensuring that the water doesn't touch the base of the bowl. Leave until the chocolate is completely melted.

2. Heat the cream, glucose and liqueur in a saucepan until the glucose has dissolved and the mixture is approximately the same temperature as the melted chocolate.

3. Pour the melted chocolate into the cream mixture and mix thoroughly with a spatula. Add the desiccated coconut and mix to evenly distribute the coconut throughout.

4. Line a small glass dish with baking parchment and pour in the mixture. Cover with clingfilm and leave in the fridge for 2 hours until set. (Once the mixture has set it can be frozen if necessary and will keep for up to 1 month. When ready to use, defrost completely and then continue with the method.)

5. Turn the mixture out of the bowl and roughly cut into 15g pieces. Roll the pieces between your palms to form balls and then roll the balls in rainbow sprinkles – the heat from your hands should make the sprinkles stick.

6. Store in an airtight container in the fridge; they will keep for up to 1 week.

Makes about 30

400g white chocolate
90ml double cream
25ml liquid glucose
25ml Malibu or other coconut liqueur
50g desiccated coconut
1 jar rainbow sprinkles

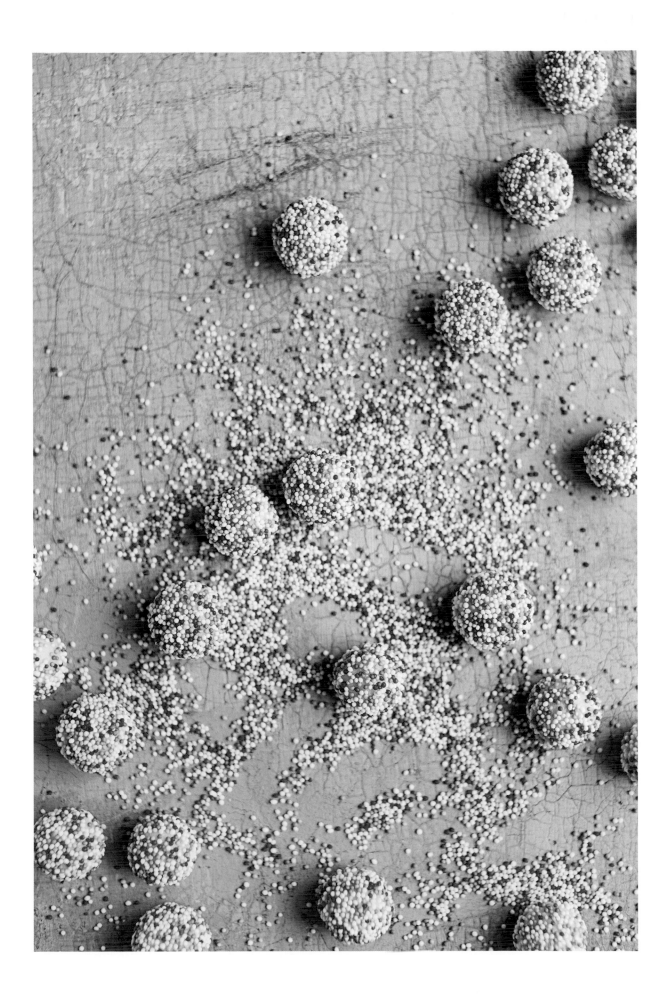

Praline Moelleux with Coffee Ice Cream

Moelleux – what a sexy name! It's a French word meaning soft, mellow, tender and MOIST, and that's exactly what this pudding is. Moelleux is normally made with chocolate, but this one has praline (hazelnuts) and is served with coffee ice cream. It's best straight from the oven with a little dusting of icing sugar so that it's hot and gooey in the centre with a soufflé-type cake around it. Mmmmmmmm...

1. Preheat the oven to 200°C/gas mark 6.

2. Whisk the egg yolks and sugar together in an electric mixer fitted with a whisk attachment until pale and fluffy.

3. In a separate bowl, mix 150g of the butter, the praline paste and the flour together, then combine with the egg yolk mixture.

4. Whisk the egg whites until soft peaks form, then fold into the praline mixture.

5. Brush the remaining softened butter inside four 7cm pastry rings and dust with the flour until completely coated. Stand the rings on a baking tray lined with greaseproof paper and fill the rings two-thirds full with the mixture. Bake for 8 minutes.

Once they are ready, serve the moelleux immediately, standing a ramekin in the centre of each serving plate. Place a spoonful of hazelnuts on each moelleux and top with a spoonful of the coffee ice cream.

Serves 4

For the praline moelleux
15 large free-range egg yolks
100g caster sugar
200g salted butter, softened
150g praline paste
2 large free-range egg whites
50g rice flour

To serve
70g toasted hazelnuts, chopped
Vanilla Ice Cream (see page 202), with
   1 tablespoon good-quality instant
   coffee granules, added at step 3

Peanut Butter Lollipops

I have had these on my menu since my first head chef job at Jessica's, and they're fab. I really should package them up and sell them - they are that popular. The base is easy too; the dipping is a little tricky, but you'll get the hang of it with practice. They are a great petit four and lovely with coffee or perfect just to have there for a fridge raid. But remember - fridge pickers wear big knickers!

1. Put the unopened cans of condensed milk into a saucepan and cover completely with water. Boil the cans for 7 hours to turn the milk to caramel, topping up the water as necessary. Remove from the heat and leave to cool in the pan. (It's best to do this 24 hours in advance.)

2. Line a flat plastic tray with silicone or greaseproof paper and place it in the freezer.

3. Mix the boiled condensed milk with the peanut butter using an electric mixer with a paddle attachment on a medium speed until fully mixed.

4. Line a casserole dish with clingfilm, spoon the mixture into the dish and cover with clingfilm. Refrigerate for 2 hours until set.

5. Turn the set mixture out onto a chopping board and cut into 10-12g pieces. Roll into balls between your palms and place the balls on a tray, then refrigerate for 30 minutes.

6. Break the chocolate into pieces and put into a glass bowl set over a saucepan of hot water over a medium heat, ensuring that the water doesn't touch the base of the bowl. Leave until the chocolate is completely melted.

7. Remove the lined plastic tray from the freezer. Using a cocktail stick, dip the peanut butter balls into the melted chocolate and stand upright on the tray. Keep the lollipops in the fridge until ready to serve. They will keep for 3 days.

Makes about 50

2 x 397g cans condensed milk
340g jar smooth peanut butter
200g dark chocolate (70% cocoa solids)

Marjoram-scented Crème Caramel

This is a French classic and sometimes it's best to leave the classics alone, so I don't really mess around with it too much. I've done more in the way of a gentle twist by infusing the milk with marjoram, which imparts a subtle flavour and gives the dish another angle. With the blackberries it's a class act, but pear makes an interesting alternative. You could also experiment by infusing the milk with different herbs.

1. Preheat the oven to 140°C/gas mark 1.

2. Pour the milk into a saucepan and add the marjoram sprigs and the seeds scraped from the vanilla pod along with the pod. Bring to the boil, then remove the pan from the heat and leave to infuse for 5 minutes.

3. Stir the eggs and 100g of the sugar together in a bowl until combined. Pass the infused milk through a sieve into a jug and then gradually whisk the warm milk into the egg mixture. Set aside.

4. Heat the water and the rest of the sugar in a heavy-based saucepan over a medium heat until the sugar has dissolved, then increase the heat slightly and bring to the boil. Every now and then, brush the sides of the pan with a pastry brush dipped in cold water to prevent sugar crystals forming. Boil for about 3-4 minutes, or until the mixture turns to a dark golden-brown caramel.

5. Immediately pour the hot caramel into four 8cm diameter, 3cm deep ramekins, carefully swirling each one so that the caramel coats the base. Leave to cool at room temperature for about 10 minutes until the caramel has set.

6. Stand the ramekins in a small roasting tin, then pour the custard into each one. Carefully add hot water to the roasting tin so that it comes halfway up the sides of the ramekins (take care not to get any water in the custard).

7. Cook in the oven for 20-30 minutes, or until just set (there should be a slight wobble in the very centre of the custard). Remove from the oven and leave to cool, then chill in the fridge, preferably overnight.

Run a blunt-ended knife around the edges of each ramekin and turn out onto serving plates, giving them a firm shake if necessary. Scatter the crushed blackberries around the edges, decorate with a few marjoram leaves and dust with icing sugar.

Serves 4

275ml full-fat milk
2 sprigs of marjoram, plus extra
  leaves to decorate
1 vanilla pod, split
2 large free-range eggs
200g caster sugar
2 tablespoons water
a handful of blackberries, lightly
  crushed (optional)
icing sugar, for dusting

White Chocolate and Crème Fraîche Truffle with Orange Syrup

I'm not a massive fan of white chocolate, but I love this because of the crème fraîche. It makes it really smooth, very rich and so moreish. It's light, but putting textures with it helps, like the crumble and tuile from the Warm Chocolate Mousse recipe (see page 152). The orange also works very well with it, although it's only there to enhance the crème fraîche. Pineapple is a great alternative to orange if you want to change things around.

1. Break the chocolate into pieces and put into a glass bowl set over a saucepan of hot water over a medium heat, ensuring that the water doesn't touch the base of the bowl. Stir the chocolate constantly until it reaches 36°C on a cooking thermometer.

2. In a separate bowl, gently whisk the crème fraîche and cream together until the mixture begins to thicken.

3. Slowly pour the melted chocolate onto the cream mixture, stirring constantly to fully incorporate the chocolate before it cools down too much - if it's not at the right temperature it will begin to set.

4. Cover with clingfilm and leave in the fridge for 2-3 hours until set.

1. Whizz the sugar and orange juice in a blender until fully combined.

2. Pour into a saucepan over a medium heat and simmer until the mixture thickens.

3. Remove from the heat and leave to cool.

Arrange a line of chocolate crumble on each serving plate and place a scoop or quenelle (see page 39) of truffle on top. Arrange shards of chocolate tuile on and around the truffle, then drizzle the dish with the orange syrup.

Serves 4

For the truffle
100g white chocolate
100ml crème fraîche
100ml double cream

For the orange syrup
20g caster sugar
240ml fresh orange juice

To serve
Chocolate Crumble (see page 152)
Chocolate Tuile (see page 152)

Burnt English Custard Egg Surprise with Marinated Strawberries, Tarragon and Black Pepper Honeycomb

One lunchtime, a table of three ordered the tasting menu, which is finished off with the Custard Egg Surprise, served on a little egg stand with a teaspoon and a plate with strawberries and honeycomb. I walked past the table and was shocked to see that they had taken the eggs off the stands, put them on the plates and smashed them to bits with spoons. They were eating everything, shell included! All three of them. WTF!
I went back to the kitchen and wasn't really sure what to do. I waited for the plates to be returned to the kitchen and then asked the waiter, 'What happened? What did they say?'
'They loved it chef.'
'But they ate the egg shells!'
'Yeah. Loved them too.'
Still can't believe it to this day.

---

1. Bring the sugar, honey, glucose and water to the boil in a saucepan. Place a sugar thermometer in the pan and boil the mixture until it reaches 150°C. (This mixture will double in volume, so make sure you use a big enough pan.)

2. Add the bicarbonate of soda and quickly whisk to combine. The mixture will rise up in the pan when the bicarb is added, so be careful.

3. Immediately pour the mixture into a non-stick baking tray. Add several grindings of black pepper and leave to cool and set for about 1 hour at room temperature, uncovered. Once set, break into shards.

1. Combine all the ingredients except the strawberries in a saucepan and gently simmer until the liquid has reduced by half.

2. Pour over the strawberries in a small bowl and leave to infuse for 30 minutes.

1. Heat the sugar and water in a heavy-based saucepan over a medium heat until the sugar has dissolved, then increase the heat slightly and bring to the boil. Every now and then, brush the sides of the pan with a pastry brush dipped in cold water to prevent sugar crystals forming. Boil for about 3–4 minutes, or until the mixture turns to a dark golden-brown caramel.

2. Pour the caramel into a greased non-stick baking tray and leave to cool and set for about 1 hour at room temperature, uncovered. Once set, shatter into small shards.

Serves 8

For the honeycomb
200g caster sugar
35g honey, preferably Solihull Heather
70ml liquid glucose
2 tablespoons water
10g bicarbonate of soda
freshly ground black pepper

For the marinated strawberries
150g caster sugar
150ml Banyuls (sweet red wine)
50ml water
3 star anise
½ bunch of tarragon
6–7 strawberries per person, hulled and halved if large

For the caramel
70g caster sugar
2 tablespoons water
sunflower oil, for greasing

continued overleaf . . .

Burnt English Custard Egg Surprise with Marinated Strawberries, Tarragon and Black Pepper Honeycomb ctd

1. Remove the tops of the eggs (this is most easily done using a special egg-top remover, available from specialist kitchenware shops or online suppliers) and pour the contents through an egg separator (available from the same sources). Set aside the egg whites for use in another recipe such as meringue (they will keep, covered, in the fridge for 2 days) and put the egg yolks in a mixing bowl. Remove the membrane from the eggshells, then clean and dry the shells.

2. Add the sugar to the bowl with the egg yolks and whisk together until pale and fluffy.

3. Pour the cream into a small saucepan and add the seeds scraped from the vanilla pods along with the pods. Heat over a gentle heat until just below boiling point, then remove from the heat, discard the vanilla pods and pour the hot cream over the egg yolks and sugar and whisk until combined.

4. Pour the mixture into a clean saucepan, return to a gentle heat and stir until it starts to thicken enough to coat the back of a spoon. Set aside and leave to cool slightly.

Carefully spoon or pipe the custard mixture into the cleaned eggshells and put them in an empty eggbox to keep them level. Sprinkle a little caramel over the custard in each egg and re-melt it using a kitchen blowtorch. Serve each egg in an eggcup on a small serving plate with the infused strawberries, decorated with the black pepper honeycomb and deep-fried tarragon leaves.

For the burnt English custard
9 large free-range eggs
85g caster sugar
500ml double cream
2 vanilla pods, split

To serve
small bunch of tarragon, deep-fried in vegetable oil until crisp, to decorate

Stocks
Pots
& Bread Rolls

The commis
and the cucumber!

As an apprentice (commis chef) you are regarded as the bottom of the pile. Years ago, when I started, you were known as dog shit! In those days, you were so far down the list you would have to pick up the rota (normally pinned to the top of a door) off the floor to see your shifts. In the pecking order it went from head chef, sous chef to - you get my drift.

Kitchens are cramped places and, when you have 40-50 men in a hot environment, things can get a bit playful. In the past, if you were a new boy, especially a commis, it was best to keep your head down. If you didn't, you could find yourself tied up and left in the freezer, dunked in a sink filled with ice-cold water, undergoing a good whipping with a leek, with your head down the toilet or, if you were really lucky, being subjected to a classic nipple twist.

In one kitchen I worked in, there was a commis - who we'll call H, as I don't want to be sued - who had pissed everyone off. One day, things came to a head. You just knew he was going to be in for it. I heard a massive noise, there was a bit of commotion and I saw the big bulls of the kitchen surround H. They dragged him into fridge number 3 - the veg fridge. I ran to see what was going on, keeping well out of sight, of course. They grabbed H, roughed him up a bit and started leek whipping him. At this point H was laughing, but when, after a couple of slaps, a chef got a cucumber and held it up like a medieval jousting stick he visibly paled. H was forceably bent over some veg boxes and the chef ran towards him . . . only to swerve and break the cucumber over one of the boxes to the side. Everyone disappeared, leaving H surrounded by broken cucumber and leeks.

The moral of the story is - keep your mouth shut and head down.

Simple White Loaf

Making bread can sometimes scare people, but believe me it's not scary. This is where you start, with a simple white loaf. It will, pardon the pun, 'raise' or grow your bread-making confidence. It's that easy kids could make it, but it could become a seriously messy business. Simply enjoy with jam or butter at a dinner party or family lunch.

1. Preheat the oven to 200°C/gas mark 6.

2. Pour the milk and the water into two separate saucepans and heat both until they reach 20°C on a cooking thermometer.

3. Whisk the yeast into the milk until it is fully dissolved and then add the water and whisk gently.

4. Put the flour and salt into an electric mixer fitted with a dough hook attachment. Mix on a low speed for 2 minutes.

5. Gradually add the yeast mixture to the flour, then increase to a medium speed and mix for 5 minutes.

6. Scrape all the dough into a clean, lightly oiled large bowl. Cover with a clean tea towel and leave in a warm place for 15 minutes.

7. Turn out the dough onto a lightly oiled surface. Knead the dough for 1 minute. Return the dough to a clean, lightly oiled bowl, then cover and leave in a warm place for a further 15 minutes.

8. Turn out the dough onto a lightly floured surface. Shape the dough into two loaf shapes and place each into a 12 x 25cm, 5cm deep, non-stick bread tin. Lightly dust with flour and slash the dough on top four times diagonally with a sharp knife. Leave to prove in a warm place for 20 minutes, or until doubled in size.

9. Bake in the oven for 10 minutes. Reduce the oven temperature to 160°C/ gas mark 3 and bake for a further 15 minutes.

10. Carefully turn out the loaves from the tins and place on a wire rack to cool.

Makes 2 loaves

200ml full-fat milk
150ml water
2 teaspoons fresh yeast, crumbled
500g strong white bread flour, plus
    extra for dusting
1½ teaspoons fine sea salt
olive oil

Focaccia

Focaccia is an Italian bread with a great flavour. I first made it at Alistair Little's on Frith Street in London's Soho. I was working there for a week-long stint alongside a guy called Johnny who was also a Brummie; you can imagine the wild time we had slap bang in the middle of Soho. The first day I walked into the kitchen it was buzzing, so straight away I jumped onto the pastry and got grafting away, and then a gent walked in and said out loud in a Northern voice, 'You must be Glynn?' 'Yes chef', I replied, going towards him to shake his hand. He in turn replied, 'My name is Alistair, but you can call me Al'. Instantly that reminded me of a song! Anyway, what a week. I learnt so much about the importance of ingredients and flavour over presentation. And what a great chef, one of Britain's best, especially of his generation, and how many chefs would agree with me on that? He showed me how to make focaccia and I still use the same method today - truly an inspirational chef. So this is from Al to me to you.

1. Put the tepid water into a bowl and whisk in the yeast until it has fully dissolved.

2. Put 250g of the flour into an electric mixer fitted with a dough hook attachment. Add the yeast mixture to the flour and mix on a medium speed until the dough is wet and sticky.

3. Remove the bowl from the mixer and scrape down any dough from the sides into the bowl. Cover the bowl with clingfilm and leave to prove in a warm place for 30-45 minutes, or until the dough has doubled in size.

4. Remove the clingfilm from the bowl and return to the mixer. Mix the salt into the remaining 250g flour, then gradually add to the dough with the mixer on a medium speed. Once completely combined, mix for 5-7 minutes.

5. Line a bread tray about 30 x 40cm with silicone or greaseproof paper and turn out the dough onto the tray. Dust with flour and then push down to flatten the dough and fill the tray completely to the edges until about 2cm in depth.

6. Brush the dough generously with rosemary oil and sprinkle with rock salt. Carefully push your fingertips into the dough to create little wells evenly across the surface. Leave to prove in a warm place for 15-25 minutes, or until the dough has doubled in size.

7. Meanwhile, preheat the oven to 190°C/gas mark 5.

8. Bake for 20-25 minutes, or until golden brown. Remove the bread from the tray and place on a wire rack to cool.

Makes 1 large loaf

350ml tepid water, 55-58°C
15g fresh yeast, crumbled
500g strong white bread flour, plus extra for dusting
15g table salt
Rosemary Oil (see page 193), for brushing
rock salt, for sprinkling

Pain de Campagne

This is great bread, which we serve in the restaurant. It's so light, you can easily eat the whole loaf. It's not brown and it's not white; it's just sick or, as I like to say, it's mustard! The bread takes a while to make, but it's a massive sense of achievement and a treat. Make it and you make people smile – just watch their little faces light up as they bite into it. At Purnell's we whip salted butter so that it's soft and spreads easily over the cloud-like texture of the bread, which works in harmony with the lovely crunch of the crust and a sprinkle of rock salt to finish.

1. Put 350ml of the tepid water into a bowl and whisk in the yeast until it has fully dissolved. Add the treacle and sunflower oil and whisk again until fully combined. Leave the mixture for 5 minutes to ferment.

2. Put the flour and salt into an electric mixer fitted with a dough hook attachment and start to mix on a slow speed.

3. While mixing, slowly pour the yeast mixture into the flour. Gradually add the extra tepid water if needed to form a smooth dough. Increase the speed to medium and beat the dough for 5 minutes.

4. Remove the bowl from the mixer and scrape any dough from the attachment and sides of the bowl using a pastry scraper. Cover the bowl with clingfilm and leave the dough to prove in a warm place for 20 minutes, or until it has doubled in size.

5. Scrape the dough from the bowl onto a lightly floured surface and lightly flour the dough. Divide the dough into four and shape each into a tight ball. Dust again with flour and cover with clingfilm. Leave to rest for 5 minutes.

6. Lightly flour four 12 x 25cm, 5cm deep, non-stick bread tins. Remove the clingfilm and shape each ball into a loaf, then place in the tins. Dust the loaves with a little flour, cover with clingfilm and leave to prove in a warm place for a further 30-40 minutes. (For a lighter dough and harder crust, place the tins in the fridge at this stage and leave for 24 hours.)

7. Meanwhile, preheat the oven to 190°C/gas mark 5.

8. Remove the clingfilm from the tins and place them on the middle shelf of the oven. Spray the inside of the oven 6-7 times with water and then bake for 12 minutes. Reduce the oven temperature to 170°C/gas mark 3 and bake for a further 10 minutes.

9. Turn out one of the loaves and gently tap the bottom – if it sounds hollow, then they are ready. Once ready, turn out all four loaves and place on a wire rack to cool for at least 15 minutes before serving.

Makes 4 loaves

350-500ml tepid water, 55-58°C
25g fresh yeast, crumbled
25g black treacle
50ml sunflower oil
450g pain de campagne flour, plus extra for dusting
15g salt
spray bottle of water

Brioche

Is this the King of Breads? It's up there with sourdough and parkin bread for me. It's so buttery, light and very versatile, I don't know anybody who doesn't like it. What's not to like, either covered with jam or even dunked into a big mug of French coffee or hot chocolate? I picked this recipe up while working in France. I shared a room with a guy called Ziggy, a chef from Iceland, in which we would drink beer and have a cheeky smoke after a busy service. Having your arse kicked by the French brigade all day, there was a sense of release knowing that the arse-kicking was going to happen all over again tomorrow. In payback we would pinch the brioche and eat it when the munchies kicked in. So from the romantic French breakfast, to the freshly toasted alongside foie gras, to the mellow nights in France – here it is, the King of Breads.

1. Put the tepid water into a bowl and whisk in the yeast until it has fully dissolved.

2. Put 450g of the flour and the sugar into an electric mixer fitted with a dough hook attachment and mix together.

3. Add the yeast mixture to the flour mixture and mix on a medium speed until the dough has fully come together, then beat the dough for 2 minutes.

4. Remove the bowl from the mixer and scrape any dough from the attachment and sides into the bowl using a pastry scraper. Cover the bowl with clingfilm and leave the dough to prove in a warm place for 30 minutes, or until the dough has doubled in size.

5. Mix together the remaining flour and salt in a bowl. Add the butter and rub in with your fingertips until you have a crumb consistency. Set aside in a cool place. Crack the eggs into a separate bowl.

6. Once the bread dough has proved, remove the clingfilm, return the bowl to the mixer and gradually add the crumbed flour mixture to the dough with the mixer on a low speed.

7. Gradually add the eggs and beat the mixture on a low speed. Once completely combined, increase the speed to a medium-high and mix for 5–7 minutes.

8. Turn out the dough onto a lightly floured surface. Separate into three batches and shape each into a loaf shape. Put into three 12 x 25cm, 5cm deep, non-stick bread tins and dust with flour. Cover each tin with clingfilm and leave to prove in a warm place for 30–40 minutes.

9. Meanwhile, preheat the oven to 190°C/gas mark 5.

10. Bake the bread for 20–25 minutes. Turn out one of the loaves and gently tap the bottom – if it sounds hollow, then they are ready. Once ready, turn out all three loaves onto a wire rack and leave to cool.

The 'retarded' dough method also works well with brioche. Once you have completed step 7, turn out the dough into a clean, lightly floured bowl twice the height of the dough. Cover tightly with clingfilm and refrigerate for 12–24 hours.

Makes 3 loaves

250ml tepid water, 55–58°C
40g fresh yeast, crumbled
850g strong white bread flour, plus
   extra for dusting
75g caster sugar
20g salt
275g salted butter, chilled and diced
6 large free-range eggs

Pikelets

Here's a row about to happen. I call them pikelets, but you may well call them crumpets, so fight away if you want.

These little gems were a Sunday evening treat for me, my brother and my sisters, mainly because we ran out of leftovers from the Sunday roast. If we were really lucky we would get to eat them in front of the telly, but more often than not we would be sat at the table, dressed in our PJs with a pot of tea or glass of milk. When I think about a pikelet, eat a pikelet or even make a pikelet, I get the wonderful feeling of home. I'm a little bit too big to wear pyjamas, but after the second pikelet I'm tempted. My kids love 'em too, although they call them crumpets because they're too young to know better. So here are my very own pikelets, or for you losers, crumpets.

1. Put the warm water into a bowl and whisk in the yeast until it has fully dissolved. Cover with clingfilm and leave in a warm place for 30 minutes to ferment.

2. In a separate bowl, mix the flour and sugar together and then whisk in the milk.

3. Beat the yeast mixture into the flour mixture to form a thick batter.

4. Preheat the oven to 180°C/gas mark 4.

5. Whisk in the baking powder and salt only when you are ready to use the batter.

6. Place a non-stick frying pan over a medium heat. Grease the inside of 7cm metal pastry rings, 3cm deep, and place them in the pan.

7. Using a ladle, half fill the rings with the batter and fry for 5 minutes, or until golden brown.

8. Carefully remove the metal rings and then turn each pikelet over and cook for a further 2 minutes.

9. Remove from the pan and place on a baking tray, then bake for 5 minutes and they are ready to serve immediately.

Makes 10

175ml warm water
7g fresh yeast, crumbled
225g strong white bread flour
½ teaspoon caster sugar
175ml full-fat milk
½ teaspoon baking powder
1 teaspoon salt
butter, for greasing

Parkin Bread

Parkin bread can be used in many different ways, as part of a dessert, with cheese or even foie gras or a creamy liver pâté. It can also be served with a rich game dish or transformed into a dark bread sauce. It's pretty easy to make, but a little different. Parkin bread is from up North and is the equivalent of the French pain d'épices. What I like about this bread, unlike the French version and just like the British in general, is that it's got a good set of bollocks, and it gives any French bread a good scrap.

1. Preheat the oven to 180°C/gas mark 4.

2. Mix the flour, spices and salt together in an electric mixer fitted with a paddle attachment on a low speed.

3. Add the oats, sugar and bicarbonate of soda and continue mixing.

4. Whisk the milk, treacle and melted butter together in a bowl and then, while the mixer is running, pour it into the dry mixture. Mix for 2 minutes.

5. Add the egg and beat for a further 2 minutes.

6. Pour the mixture into two 12 x 25cm, 5cm deep, non-stick bread tins and immediately bake for 20-25 minutes.

7. Place a knife in the centre of each loaf – if it comes out clean then they are done. Turn out the loaves from the tins and place on a wire rack to cool.

Makes 2 loaves

175g strong white bread flour, plus extra for dusting
2 teaspoons ground ginger
1 teaspoon ground cinnamon
1 teaspoon freshly grated nutmeg
1 teaspoon salt
275g jumbo porridge oats
110g dark muscovado sugar
1 teaspoon bicarbonate of soda
150ml full-fat milk, warmed
175g black treacle
150g salted butter, melted
1 large free-range egg

Waffles

Great touch instead of bread, or lovely as a pud with fruit and cream - it's your choice. Like I've said, this is your cookbook written by me, so you do as you please. This is a really cool recipe for which you ideally need a waffle iron, but you can pan-fry them instead, obviously in a pan.

I like to serve them with meat and soft butter, using the waffles to soak up the juices, or take your cue from the wise words of Donkey from the movie *Shrek*: 'This is going to be fun; we can stay up late swappin' manly stories and in the morning I'm making waffles!' As recommended by Donkey, you can have them for breakfast; with poached eggs and a couple of rashers of bacon, they're amazing. I have covered the lot now - breakfast, snack, dinner or even pud - so I'll stop waffling on (shit joke, but hey, it's only a cookbook) and you can go and make some.

---

1. Cook the potatoes in a saucepan of lightly boiling water for 20-25 minutes, or until fork tender. Strain off all the water and then break up the potatoes with a fork to a rough consistency. Set aside.

2. Mix the flour, baking powder and salt together in a large bowl.

3. In a separate bowl, combine the potatoes with the milk, sugar and melted butter. Stir into the flour mixture and beat well to form a batter.

4. Whisk the egg whites until stiff peaks form, then fold into the batter a third at a time. The batter will be thick.

5. Lightly grease a waffle iron with spray cooking oil and heat until medium hot. Ladle in the batter, ensuring that you don't overfill the waffle iron, then close the lid and cook for 5-6 minutes, or until pale golden brown. Remove from the iron and serve immediately, or keep warm in the oven while you repeat with the remaining batter.

Makes 20

265g potatoes, peeled and cubed
200g strong white bread flour
1 tablespoon baking powder
½ teaspoon salt
225ml full-fat milk
25g soft light brown sugar
60g butter, melted
6 large free-range egg whites
spray cooking oil, for greasing

Gougères

Historically, gougères were served cold when tasting wine in the cellars of Burgundy, but they can be eaten warm. Many restaurants present them before the meal with an aperitif. I did the same in the past in this way, but sometimes I like to serve gougères as a starter pumped with hot, rich cheese sauce. Choux is a fantastic pastry and really lends itself to kicking things off as a nibble with pre-dinner drinks or as part of a starter. They are really light, but truly delicious.

Makes 50

360ml water
145g salted butter, diced
120g Parmesan cheese, grated
15g salt
290g strong white bread flour
6 large free-range eggs

1. Preheat the oven to 180°C/gas mark 4.

2. Bring the water, butter, 100g of the Parmesan and the salt to the boil in a large saucepan.

3. Gradually add the flour to the pan, stirring constantly. Cook over a medium heat, stirring, for 5 minutes until smooth.

4. Transfer the mixture to an electric mixer fitted with a paddle attachment and beat on a slow speed for 2 minutes.

5. Add the eggs, one at a time, and beat for a further 5 minutes.

6. Transfer the mixture to a piping bag fitted with a medium round piping nozzle. (The mixture can be frozen at this point and kept for up to 1 month. Simply defrost before continuing with the method.)

7. Pipe 1.5-2cm balls of the choux mixture onto a baking tray lined with greaseproof paper. Allow a 2cm gap in between. Sprinkle with the remainder of the Parmesan.

8. Bake for 15 minutes, or until risen and golden brown. Leave to cool on the baking tray.

Foie Gras Butter

Get this, to make foie gras butter you need foie gras, but you know what, I can't believe... there is no butter! And when you make this you won't believe it either. You'll be spreading it on everything... even your other half.

250g high-quality foie gras lobe
1 teaspoon Chinese four-spice powder
1 teaspoon salt, plus extra for seasoning if necessary
15ml good-quality Armagnac or brandy

1. Preheat the oven to 220°C/gas mark 7.

2. Leave the foie gras at room temperature for 3 hours prior to preparation.

3. Lay a sheet of silicone or greaseproof paper on a baking tray and flatten the foie gras onto it. Make indentations with your fingertips all over it.

4. Sprinkle with the four-spice and salt and spread evenly, then pour the Armagnac or brandy over and spread evenly.

5. Place in the oven for 2 minutes – do not overcook because this will cause the foie gras to become grainy.

6. Pass the foie gras through a fine sieve into a mixing bowl and then whisk it constantly while it cools until it reaches the consistency of butter. Season with salt if necessary.

Pistachio Gnocchi

Gnocchi is a brilliant addition to a meat or fish dish. It's a pasta of sorts, with potato, which will cover all bases. Adding the pistachio nut brings it to another level elevating the flavour and giving it a makeover. It is cool as an accompaniment or on its own as a little afternoon dish, but for me the pleasure is in the making. People think that gnocchi is difficult to make, so, when you serve it with a glass or two, you will look the pistachios!...............(nuts)

1. Preheat the oven to 180°C/gas mark 4.

2. Sprinkle the salt on a baking tray and sit the potatoes on top. Bake for about 45 minutes, or until the potatoes are soft.

3. Remove from the oven and, while they are still hot, scoop out the flesh and pass through a fine sieve. Put 500g of the potato into a bowl.

4. Mix together the flour, semolina, Parmesan, pistachios and white pepper and nutmeg to taste, then add to the potato and mix together. Mix in the egg yolk and finally add the melted butter.

5. Roll the mixture between your palms into 2cm balls and press down firmly on top with a fork to create a disk shape.

6. Blanch in a saucepan of salted boiling water until the gnocchi float to the surface of the water, then drain well.

7. Heat the knob of butter in a frying pan until foaming, then add the gnocchi and cook, turning frequently, for about 2 minutes until lightly coloured.

Serves 16

200g salt, plus extra for blanching the gnocchi
4 large potatoes
125g strong white bread flour
50g semolina
50g Parmesan cheese, grated
100g shelled skinned pistachio nuts, ground, plus extra to garnish
freshly ground white pepper
freshly ground nutmeg, to taste
1 large free-range egg yolk
10g butter, melted, plus an extra knob for pan-frying the gnocchi

STOCKS

Beef Stock

1. Preheat the oven to 200°C/gas mark 6.

2. Place the bones in a roasting tin and roast for 20-30 minutes, stirring occasionally to get an even colour. Remove from the oven, lift out the bones and set aside.

3. Cut the garlic bulb in half horizontally to expose all the cloves, then place, cut side down, in the roasting tin along with all the vegetables and return to the oven for 10 minutes, or until evenly coloured.

4. Remove from the oven and transfer the contents to a stock pot with the roasted bones, thyme and bay leaf. Pour over the water and bring up to a gentle simmer over a medium heat.

5. Put the roasting tin on the hob and deglaze with the red wine, scraping up the sediment on the base of the tin with a wooden spoon. Add the wine to the stock and simmer gently for 4 hours, frequently skimming off any impurities from the surface.

6. Pass the stock through a fine sieve and leave to cool. Cover and refrigerate; the fat will solidify and then be easy to remove.

Makes 3 litres

1kg veal or beef bones, chopped
1 garlic bulb
2 carrots, peeled and roughly chopped
2 onions, peeled and roughly chopped
3 celery sticks, roughly chopped
4 tomatoes, roughly chopped
2 field mushrooms, roughly chopped
½ bunch of thyme
bay leaf
2 litres water
½ bottle (375ml) of red wine

Chicken Stock

1. Put the chicken bones and wings into a large saucepan and cover with water. Bring to the boil and then simmer for 10 minutes. Skim off any impurities from the surface.

2. Add the remainder of the ingredients and simmer for 20 minutes, frequently skimming the surface.

3. Pass through a fine sieve and leave to cool. Cover and refrigerate.

Makes 3 litres

1kg chicken bones, chopped
6 chicken wings
2 onions, peeled and chopped
1 leek, chopped
4 celery sticks, chopped
3 carrots, peeled and chopped
3 bay leaves
10 black peppercorns
½ garlic bulb
½ bunch of thyme
2 tomatoes
2 tablespoons curry powder

Fish Sauce

1. Heat the sunflower oil in a large saucepan over a high heat, add the fish bones and cook until caramelised, using a wooden spoon to constantly scrape all the fish sediment that sticks to the base of the pan. Tip the contents of the pan into a bowl and set aside.

2. Deglaze pan with the apple juice and return the fish bones to the pan. Just cover with water and bring to a gentle simmer. Add the vegetables and gently simmer for 45 minutes.

3. Strain off the fish stock through a fine sieve into a medium saucepan and simmer over a medium heat until reduced to a sauce consistency.

4. Finish sauce the sauce with a knob of butter and squeeze of lemon juice. Keep warm until needed.

The sauce is a perfect accompaniment to a fish main course.

Makes 500ml

1 tablespoon sunflower oil
1kg fish bones (turbot and brill are the best), chopped
400ml apple juice
1 leek, finely sliced
1 onion, peeled and finely sliced
2 celery sticks, finely sliced
small knob of unsalted butter
squeeze of lemon juice

Crispy Fish Skin

1. Preheat the oven to 180°C/gas mark 4.

2. Lay the fish skin on a sheet of silicone or greaseproof paper on a flat baking tray and brush with the clarified butter.

3. Place another sheet of silicone or greaseproof paper over the skin and another baking tray on top to keep the skin flat. Bake for 15 minutes, or until crispy.

4. Remove from the oven and, while still warm, season to taste with sea salt and ginger. Leave to cool before using.

The skin can be used as a garnish for a starter or main course. It could also be used in a salad.

Makes 4 portions

1 large flat fish skin (cod, pollack or hake) washed, descaled and dried
50g clarified salted butter, melted
sea salt
ground ginger, to taste

Red Wine Gravy

1. Heat the oil in a large saucepan, add the shallots and garlic and cook over a medium heat until caramelised. Add the tomatoes, thyme and peppercorns and sweat for 5 minutes.

2. Add the red wine, cook until reduced to a glaze, then add the beef stock.

3. Reduce the sauce down to 250ml, remove from the stove and whisk in two pieces of butter at a time until all the butter is completely emulsified; if the sauce comes back to the boil and splits, allow the sauce to cool and whisk until it emulsifies. Whisk in the lemon juice just before serving.

Serves 4

splash of vegetable oil
2 shallots, peeled and finely sliced
2 garlic cloves, peeled and finely sliced
2 tomatoes, quartered
4 sprigs of thyme
1 teaspoon black peppercorns
400ml red wine
1 litre good quality beef stock (see basics)
100g butter, diced
2 teaspoons fresh lemon juice

Mayonnaise

1. Add the mustard and vinegar to the yolks and whisk thoroughly to emulsify.

2. While constantly whisking, slowly pour the oil at a constant rate into the egg mixture and continue to whisk until the oil is completely incorporated and a mayonnaise consistency is achieved.

3. Season to taste with salt and ginger, then place in an airtight container, seal and refrigerate.

For lemon mayonnaise
Add lemon juice to taste

Makes 500g

3 large free-range egg yolks
1 teaspoon Dijon mustard
2 teaspoons white wine vinegar
400ml sunflower oil
salt
ground ginger, to taste

Vinaigrette

Whisk the oil and vinegar together in a bowl, then whisk in the salt, black pepper and lime juice.

Makes 500ml

400ml rapeseed oil (or use sunflower or light olive oil)
100ml Chardonnay vinegar (or use good-quality white wine vinegar)
pinch of salt
2 turns of a black pepper mill
squeeze of lime juice

OILS

Curry Oil

1. Warm the sunflower oil in a saucepan over a medium heat until it reaches about 60°C on a cooking thermometer.

2. Add the curry powder to the oil and leave to infuse over the heat for 20 minutes, then remove from the heat and leave to cool.

3. Once cool, pour into a bowl, cover and leave to steep for 24 hours.

4. Pass through a muslin cloth, then use as required. Store in bottles or kilner jars at room temperature.

Makes 200ml

200ml sunflower oil
50g curry powder

Rosemary Oil

1. Warm the sunflower oil in a saucepan over a medium heat until it reaches about 60°C on a cooking thermometer.

2. Add the rosemary sprigs to the oil, remove from the heat and leave to cool.

3. Once cool, pour into a bowl, cover and leave to steep for 24 hours.

4. Pass through a fine sieve, then use as required. Store in bottles or kilner jars at room temperature.

Makes 150ml

150ml sunflower oil
5 sprigs of rosemary

Parsley Oil

1. Bring the water and salt to a rolling boil in a large saucepan.

2. Blanch the parsley in the boiling water for 20 seconds and immediately refresh in a bowl of iced water.

3. Drain and squeeze the excess water out of the parsley. Place the parsley and half the oil in a blender and whizz, while slowly adding the remainder of the oil. Once all the oil is added, whizz for a further 6 minutes.

4. Transfer the mixture to a clean bowl, cover and leave to steep for 24 hours.

5. Pass through a muslin cloth, then use as required. Store in bottles or kilner jars at room temperature.

Makes 350ml

5 litres water
200g salt
500g flatleaf parsley
500ml sunflower oil

Basil Oil

1. Add the salt to a litre of water and bring to the boil..

2. Blanch the basil in the water for 15 seconds and then refresh in iced water.

3. Squeeze out any excess water, add to a blender along with the sunflower oil and blend for 5 minutes.

4. Tip into a container, cover and leave to steep for 24 hours. Store in bottles or kilner jars at room temperature.

Makes 150ml

75g salt
200g basil
200ml sunflower oil

Confit Cherry Tomatoes

1. Fill a medium saucepan with water and bring to the boil.

2. Use a sharp knife to score a small cross in the bottom of each tomato. In batches of five, drop the tomatoes into the boiling water for 10 seconds, and then remove with a slotted spoon and place straight into iced water. Carefully peel the tomatoes, taking care not to puncture them.

3. Melt the butter in a wide saucepan. When fully melted, add the sugar and allow to dissolve over a medium heat. Once the sugar has fully dissolved, carefully add the tomatoes to the pan along with the thyme. Cook over a low heat for 30 minutes.

4. Leave to cool slightly and serve warm.

Serves 4

20 cherry tomatoes
500g salted butter
120g dark muscovado sugar
sprig of thyme

Purnell's Masala Spice Mix

1. Put all the spices into a food processor, breaking up the cinnamon stick, and whizz for about 1 minute until nicely broken up.

2. Using a coffee grinder, grind 2 tablespoons of the mixture at a time for 10 seconds, ensuring that the grinder doesn't get too hot.

3. Pass the spice mix through a fine sieve with a ladle and store in a Kilner jar or other airtight jar.

Makes 110g

38g fenugreek seeds
20g cinnamon stick
10g fennel seeds
33g black mustard seeds
4g cloves
13g coriander seeds
28g cumin seeds

Pickling Liquor

1. Mix the vinegar and sugar together in a small saucepan and heat until the sugar has dissolved.

2. Remove from the heat and leave to cool, then use as required.

Makes 350ml

300ml white wine vinegar
300g granulated sugar

Pickled Cucumber

1. Put the cucumber slices into an airtight, non-reactive container with the pickling liquor, ensuring that the slices are fully submerged.

2. Leave in the fridge for a minimum of 24 hours before use. Will keep for 1 month.

Makes 10 portions

1 cucumber, peeled and cut into 1cm-thick slices
Pickling Liquor (see above) - enough to fill the container

SORBETS

Stock Syrup

1. Heat the water and sugar in a saucepan and simmer until the sugar has dissolved.

2. Remove the pan from the heat and pass the syrup through a sieve. Store in a sterilised airtight container in the fridge until needed – it will last for up to 1 month.

Serves 8

800ml water
500g caster sugar

Strawberry Sorbet

1. Put the strawberries into a saucepan, add the water and icing sugar and bring to the boil. Reduce the heat and simmer for 5 minutes, or until the strawberries are soft and mushy.

2. Pass the mixture through a sieve, then put the strawberry pulp into a blender and whizz until smooth. With the machine running, gradually add the strawberry liquor until the mixture is completely smooth and coats the back of a spoon.

3. Whisk the strawberry mixture with the stock syrup and then churn in an ice-cream machine according to the manufacturer's instructions until it reaches a sorbet consistency. Transfer to a freezerproof container and store in the freezer until needed – it will keep for up to 6 months.

Serves 8

500g strawberries, hulled and
    quartered
50ml water
1 teaspoon icing sugar
110ml Stock Syrup (see above)

Rhubarb Sorbet

1. Put the rhubarb and cranberry juice into a saucepan and bring to the boil. Reduce the heat and simmer for 5–10 minutes, or until the rhubarb is tender.

2. Pass the mixture through a sieve, then put the rhubarb pulp into a blender and whizz until smooth. With the machine running, gradually add the rhubarb liquor until the mixture is completely smooth and coats the back of a spoon.

3. Whisk the rhubarb mixture with the stock syrup and then churn in an ice-cream machine according to the manufacturer's instructions until it reaches a sorbet consistency. Transfer to a freezerproof container and store in the freezer until needed – it will keep for up to 6 months.

Serves 8

600g rhubarb, cut into large pieces
200ml cranberry juice
140ml Stock Syrup (see above)

Mango and Rosewater Sorbet

Using mango purée

1. Mix the mango purée with the stock syrup and rosewater.

2. Churn the mixture in an ice-cream machine according to the manufacturer's instructions until it reaches a sorbet consistency. Transfer to a freezerproof container and store in the freezer until needed – it will keep for up to 6 months.

Using fresh mangoes

1. Gently heat the mango flesh with the stock syrup in a saucepan until soft. Put into a blender with the rosewater and whizz until smooth, then pass through a sieve.

2. Churn and store as above.

Serves 8

500g mango purée (or 4 ripe mangoes, skinned, stoned and roughly chopped)
120g Stock Syrup (see page 198)
1 teaspoon rosewater

Pineapple Sorbet

1. Put the poached pineapple and poaching liquor in a blender and whizz until smooth, then whisk with the stock syrup.

2. Churn the mixture in an ice-cream machine according to the manufacturer's instructions until it reaches a sorbet consistency. Transfer to a freezerproof container and store in the freezer until needed – it will keep for up to 6 months.

Serves 8

400g poached pineapple (see page 128, Pineapple Upside Down Cake)
100ml strained pineapple poaching liquor (see page 128 as above)
100ml Stock Syrup (see page 198)

Apple Sorbet

1. Combine all the ingredients in a saucepan and bring to the boil.

2. Pass through a fine sieve and leave to cool.

3. Once cool, churn the mixture in an ice cream machine following the manufacturer's instructions, until it reaches a sorbet consistency. Transfer to a freezerproof container and store in the freezer until needed – it will keep for up to 6 months.

Serves 8

1 litre of good quality apple juice
300g caster sugar
300g liquid glucose

Vanilla Ice Cream

1. Place a large bowl half filled with ice and water in the fridge with a smaller bowl in the centre of it.

2. Bring the cream, milk and vanilla pods to the boil in a saucepan. Remove from the heat and leave to infuse for 20 minutes.

3. Whisk the sugar and egg yolks together in a bowl until pale and fluffy.

4. Pour the cream mixture into the yolks and whisk until fully combined. Wash the saucepan and dry thoroughly. Pour the mixture back into the saucepan and heat over a medium heat, stirring constantly with a heatproof spatula, until the mixture is thick enough to coat the back of the spatula.

5. Remove the bowls from the fridge. Pass the mixture through a fine sieve into the bowl over the iced water and stir until cool.

6. Churn the mixture in an ice-cream machine according to the manufacturer's instructions until almost set. Transfer to a freezerproof container and store in the freezer until needed – it will keep for up to 1 month.

Serves 8

300ml double cream
300ml full-fat milk
2 vanilla pods, split
85g caster sugar
6 large free-range egg yolks

Candied Zest

1. Remove the zest of the orange using a peeler. Remove any pith from the zest. Finely slice length ways into thin strips.

2. Mix 250g of caster sugar with the water in a small saucepan and stir to dissolve. Add the zest to the saucepan and place on the hob. Using a sugar thermometer bring the mixture up to 105°C..

3. Pass the mixture through a fine sieve and discard the liquid..

4. Place 250g caster sugar into a large bowl. Add the zest to the sugar, in three stages and each time toss the zest to ensure that it is fully coated in sugar. Leave to cool in the sugar.

5. Once cool, remove the zest from the bowl and store in an airtight container, this will keep for four days.

Serves 8

1 large orange (alternatively you
   could use most citrus fruits)
250g caster sugar
100ml water
250g caster sugar

LEATHERS

Mango Leather

1. Preheat the oven to 70°C.

2. Put the mango and plums with the honey into a saucepan and cook over a gentle heat, stirring frequently, until soft and mushy.

3. Transfer the mixture to a blender and whizz until smooth, then pass through a fine sieve onto a sheet of silicone or greaseproof paper and spread with a palette knife until 2mm thick.

4. Slide the paper onto a baking tray and leave the fruit mixture in the oven for 4-6 hours until dry.

5. Remove from the oven and leave to cool. Cut into eighths and store in an airtight container in a cool, dry place. The leather will keep for up to 4 weeks.

Serves 10

1 ripe mango, skinned, stoned and roughly chopped
3 plums, skinned, stoned and roughly chopped
30g runny honey

Strawberry/Raspberry Leather

Follow the method above.

Serves 10

200g hulled strawberries or raspberries
25g caster sugar
4g citric acid
4 tablespoons water

Index

a

almond and Szechuan pepper poached peaches 60-61

apple
capers and shrimps with roast pork belly 114-115
pickled, lemon mayonnaise and smoked paprika honeycomb with crab salad 70-71
sorbet 201
stuffed baked, with spiced mascarpone 134-135

asparagus
English, and scallop, salad of, with cockle tartare and mint oil 85
in salted butter, with asparagus custard and chicken cooked in hay 98-99

b

Bakewell tarts with double cream ice cream and instant fruit jam 131-133
baklava, lamb, with courgette purée 116
barley, crispy, chive oil and crème fraîche with leek and potato soup 24-25

basil
oil 194
oil, tomato sorbet and tomato tartare 38-39
and tamarillo jam, with lemon and lime posset 140-141

beef
blue steak with egg and salsify chips 107
carpaccio, red wine octopus and sweet and sour onions 46-48
chunky mulligatawny 21
consommé, `Birmingham Soup' 1793 18-20
roast tail fillet of, with braised and stuffed celery and celeriac purée 110-111
short rib of, with mussels, parsley and wild garlic 108-109
stock 188
see also corned beef

beetroot mousse with escabeche of vegetables 44-45
`Birmingham Soup' 1793 18-20
black olive, rabbit and pea trifle with rabbit lollipops 55-56

black pepper
honeycomb, marinated strawberries and tarragon with burnt English custard egg surprise 126, 165-167
and malt vinegar glaze 122-123
oil 47-48

black pudding
crumble and egg 28-29
Purnell's 26

blackberry and vanilla baked cheesecake 139
blackcurrant purée, cassis pâte de fruits 142
bone marrow, smoked, `Birmingham Soup' 1793 18-20
Bosi, Claude 8, 12, 17, 36, 98

bread
brioche 176-177
focaccia 173
pain de campagne 174-175
Parkin 180-181
simple white loaf 172
breadcrumbs, pauper's cake 154
brill with toffee and cumin carrots 84
brioche 176-177
mushroom, with duck egg yolk and hollandaise 30-31
brownies, chocolate, with peaches cooked in muscovado and cava 155
burnt English custard egg surprise with marinated strawberries, tarragon and black pepper honeycomb 126, 165-167
butter, foie gras 185
butter bean, goats' cheese and chorizo, with one-pot pollack 88-89
butternut squash, orange, Szechuan pepper and truffled feta terrine 16-17
butterscotch sauce 128-130

c

cabbage, winter, salad, with posh sausage roll 33

cakes
pauper's 154
pineapple upside down 128-130
candied zest 202
capers, shrimp and apple with roast pork belly 114-115
carbon monoxide poisoning 42
carpaccio, beef, red wine octopus and sweet and sour onions 46-48

carrot
pickled, red lentils and coconut garnish, with monkfish masala 80-82
toffee and cumin, with brill 84
cassis pâte de fruits 142
caviar cream, with pan-fried sea bass `heaven and earth' 76-77
celeriac purée and braised and stuffed celery with roast tail fillet of beef 110-111
celery, braised and stuffed 110-111
Chantilly cream, warm cherries and toasted pistachios with pavlova 136-138
charcuterie sauce and sauerkraut with glazed pork chops 112-113
Cheddar custard, baked with onion salad 54

cheese
gougères 184-185
and pineapple `soixante-dix', the emotions of 49-51
sauce 49-51
see also specific cheeses
cheesecake, baked vanilla and blackberry 139
cherry, warm, toasted pistachios and Chantilly cream with pavlova 136-138

chicken
cooked in hay, with asparagus in salted butter and asparagus custard 98-99
Purnell's white pudding 27
stock 188
thighs, with pea custard and pea salad 100-101
chilli sauce, with crispy pork-covered squid 74-75

chips, salsify, egg and blue steak 107

chive
crème fraîche 46-48
oil 24-25

chocolate
brownies, with peaches cooked in muscovado and cava 155
and passion fruit domes 147-149
tuile 152-153
warm mousse, with chocolate crumble and mint ice cream 152-153
see also white chocolate

chorizo
butter beans and goats' cheese, with one-pot pollack 88-89
rabbit and foie gras terrine with raw fennel salad 58-59
choux pastry, gougères 184-185
cockle tartare and mint oil with salad of English asparagus and scallop 85

coconut
garnish 82
rice, with roasted spiced lamb 117
risotto, with lobster pistachio kebabs 72
and white chocolate ganache 156-157

cod
pan-fried roasted, with confit lemon and zhoug `my way' 91
roast, with wild horseradish 90
coffee ice cream with praline moelleux 158-159
confit cherry tomatoes 194
coriander and cucumber with spiced potted shrimps 73
corned beef `OXO' with GP sauce 52-53
cornflake, baked, From mum to Michelin 34-37
crab salad with lemon mayonnaise, smoked paprika honeycomb and pickled apples 70-71

cream
caviar 76-77
Chantilly 136-138
double cream ice cream 131-133
mustard 22-23
crème caramel, marjoram-scented 162-163

crème fraîche
chive 46-48
crispy barley and chive oil with leek and potato soup 24-25
scorched lettuce and fondue of onion with turbot 86-87
and white chocolate truffle with orange syrup 164
crumpets 178-179

cucumber
charred and pickled, cucumber sorbet and curry cured salmon 62-63
and coriander with spiced potted shrimps 73
pickled 196-197
cumin and toffee carrots with brill 84
curly kale, sweet and sour parsnips and juniper berries with roast loin of venison 120-121
curry cured salmon, charred and pickled cucumber and cucumber sorbet 62-63
curry oil 34-36, 193

custard
asparagus 98-99

baked Cheddar, with onion salad 54
burnt English, egg surprise, with
 marinated strawberries, tarragon
 and black pepper honeycomb 126,
 165-167
pea 56, 100-101

d
duck with tamarind jam, liquorice purée
 and green beans 106

e
egg
 and black pudding crumble 28-29
 duck, yolk, and hollandaise with
  mushroom brioche 30-31
 From mum to Michelin 34-37
 poached yolk and butter, potato
  cooked in, with watercress and salad
  of shrimps 32
 salsify chips and blue steak 107
 surprise, burnt English custard, with
  marinated strawberries, tarragon
  and black pepper honeycomb 126,
  165-167
emotions of cheese and pineapple
 `soixante-dix', The 49-51
escabeche of vegetables with beetroot
 mousse 44-45

f
faggots with mushy peas, onion gravy
 and malt vinegar and black pepper
 glaze 122-123
fennel, raw salad, with rabbit, foie gras
 and chorizo terrine 58-59
feta, truffled, butternut squash, orange
 and Szechuan pepper terrine 16-17
fish
 crispy skin 189
 sauce 189
 see also specific fish
focaccia 173
foie gras
 butter 185
 chorizo and rabbit terrine with raw
  fennel salad 58-59
 wrapped in kataifi, with peaches
  poached in Szechuan pepper and
  almonds 60-61
fondue of onion, crème fraîche and
 scorched lettuce with turbot 86-87
frangipane 131-133
fritters, sweetcorn 104-105
From mum to Michelin 34-37

g
ganache, white chocolate and coconut
 156-157
garlic, wild, and parsley sauce 108-109
gnocchi, pistachio 186-187
goat's cheese
 chorizo and butter beans, with one-
  pot pollack 88-89
 the emotions of cheese and pineapple
  `soixante-dix' 49-51
gougères 50, 184-185
GP sauce, with corned beef `OXO' 52-53
gravy
 onion 122-123
 red wine 189
green bean, tamarind jam and liquorice

purée with duck 106

h
haddock, smoked, foam, From mum to
 Michelin 34-37
ham hock, easy peasy soup 22-23
hay, chicken cooked in, with asparagus
 in salted butter and asparagus custard
 98-99
hollandaise and duck egg yolk with
 mushroom brioche 30-31
honeycomb
 black pepper, marinated strawberries
  and tarragon with burnt English
  custard egg surprise 126, 165-167
 smoked paprika, pickled apples, lemon
  mayonnaise and crab salad 70-71
horseplay 50
horseradish, wild, with roast cod 90

i
ice cream
 coffee 158-159
 double cream 131-133
 mint 152-153
 vanilla 202

j
jam
 instant fruit 131-133
 tamarillo and basil 140-141
 tamarind 106
Jerusalem artichoke purée, vanilla and
 roasted stem broccoli with red mullet
 92-93
juniper berry, curly kale and sweet and
 sour parsnips with roast loin of
 venison 120-121

k
kataifi, foie gras wrapped in, with
 peaches poached in Szechuan pepper
 and almonds 60-61
kebabs, lobster pistachio, with coconut
 risotto 72

l
lamb
 baklava, with courgette purée 116
 braised elbow of (shoulder shanks),
  with red lentil stew and parsley salad
  118-119
 roasted spiced, with coconut rice 117
leathers
 mango 204
 strawberry/raspberry 203
leek
 and potato soup, with crème fraîche,
  crispy barley and chive oil 24-25
 scorched 86-87
lemon
 confit, zhoug `my way' and pan-fried
  roasted cod 91
 and lime posset, with tamarillo and
  basil jam 140-141
 mayonnaise 70-71, 190
 pauper's cake 154
 shortbread 150
lemon verbena panna cotta with
 poached rhubarb, rhubarb sorbet and
 sweet toasted seeds 144-146
lentil, red

pickled carrots and coconut garnish,
 with monkfish masala 80-82
stew, and parsley salad with braised
 elbow of lamb (shoulder shanks)
 118-119
lettuce, scorched, fondue of onion and
 crème fraîche with turbot 86-87
lime and lemon posset with tamarillo
 and basil jam 140-141
liquorice purée, green beans and
 tamarind jam with duck 106
loaf, simple white 172
lobster 68
 pistachio kebabs, with coconut risotto
  72
lollipops
 peanut butter 160-161
 rabbit 55-56

m
mackerel and potato pakoras 78-79
mango
 leather 203
 and rosewater sorbet 201
marjoram scented crème caramel
 162-163
marshmallow 143
 pineapple 49-51
 Purnell's spice mix 194
mascarpone, spiced, with stuffed baked
 apple 134-135
mayonnaise 190
 lemon 70-71
meringue 136-138
mince pie roll 151
mint ice cream and chocolate crumble
 with chocolate warm mousse 152-153
mint oil and cockle tartare with salad of
 English asparagus and scallop 85
moelleux, praline, with coffee ice cream
 158-159
monkfish masala with red lentils,
 pickled carrots and coconut garnish
 80-82
mousse
 beetroot, with escabeche of
  vegetables 44-45
 red cabbage, with pickled red cabbage
  64-65
 warm chocolate, with chocolate
  crumble and mint ice cream 152-153
mulligatawny, chunky 21
mushroom brioche with duck egg yolk
 and hollandaise 30-31
mussel, parsley and wild garlic with
 short rib of beef 108-109
mustard cream 22-23
my time with Glynn, Clause Bosi 36

o
octopus, red wine, sweet and sour
 onions and beef carpaccio 46-48
oils 192-194
 basil 38-39, 194
 black pepper 47-48
 chive 24-25
 curry 34-36, 193
 mint 85
 parsley 193
 rosemary 193
olive, black, rabbit and pea trifle with
 rabbit lollipops 55-56

onion
  fondue of, crème fraîche and scorched lettuce with turbot 86-87
  gravy, malt vinegar and black pepper glaze and mushy peas with faggots 122-123
  pickled 46-48
  salad, with baked Cheddar custard 54
  sweet and sour, beef carpaccio and red wine octopus 46-48
orange
  oil 16-17
  pauper's cake 154
  syrup, with white chocolate and crème fraîche truffle 164
  Szechuan pepper, truffled feta and butternut squash terrine 16-17
ox cheek, 'Birmingham Soup' 1793 18-20

p

pain de campagne 174-175
pakoras, mackerel and potato 78-79
panna cotta, lemon verbena, with poached rhubarb, rhubarb sorbet and sweet toasted seeds 144-146
paprika, smoked, honeycomb, pickled apples, lemon mayonnaise and crab salad 70-71
Parkin bread 180-181
Parmesan cheese, gougères 184-185
parsley
  oil 193
  salad 22-23
  salad, and red lentil stew with braised elbow of lamb (shoulder shanks) 118-119
  and wild garlic sauce, with mussels and short rib of beef 108-109
parsnip, sweet and sour, juniper berries and curly kale with roast loin of venison 120-121
passion fruit and chocolate domes 147-149
pauper's cake 154
pavlova with warm cherries, toasted pistachios and Chantilly cream 136-138
pea
  custard, and pea salad with chicken thighs 100-101
  easy peasy soup 22-23
  mushy, onion gravy and malt vinegar and black pepper glaze with faggots 122-123
  salad, black olive and rabbit trifle with rabbit lollipops 55-56
peach
  cooked in muscovado and cava, with chocolate brownies 155
  poached in Szechuan pepper and almonds, with foie gras wrapped in kataifi 60-61
peanut butter lollipops 160-161
pheasant 'Maryland' 104-105
pickles
  pickled apple 70-71
  pickled carrot 80-82
  pickled cucumber 196-197
  pickled onion 46-48
  pickled red cabbage 64-65
  pickling liquor 197
pig fry (liver and heart), faggots with mushy peas, onion gravy and malt

vinegar and black pepper glaze 122-123
pig's blood, Purnell's black pudding 26
pig's trotter
  Purnell's black pudding 26
  Purnell's white pudding 27
pikelets 178-179
pineapple
  dried 50-51
  marshmallow 49-51
  sorbet 201
  upside down cake 128-130
pistachio
  gnocchi 186-187
  lobster kebabs, with coconut risotto 72
  toasted, Chantilly cream and warm cherries with pavlova 136-138
pollack, one-pot, with chorizo, butter beans and goats' cheese 88-89
pork
  crispy, -covered squid, with chilli sauce 74-75
  glazed chop, with sauerkraut and charcuterie sauce 112-113
pork back fat
  Purnell's black pudding 26
  Purnell's white pudding 27
pork belly
  faggots with mushy peas, onion gravy and malt vinegar and black pepper glaze 122-123
  roast, with shrimps, apple and capers 114-115
posset, lemon and lime, with tamarillo and basil jam 140-141
potato
  cooked in butter, poached egg yolk, with watercress and salad of shrimps 32
  and leek soup, with crème fraîche, crispy barley and chive oil 24-25
  and mackerel pakoras 78-79
praline moelleux with coffee ice cream 158-159

r

rabbit
  foie gras and chorizo terrine with raw fennel salad 58-59
  pea and black olive trifle with rabbit lollipops 55-56
raspberry leather 203
red cabbage mousse with pickled red cabbage 64-65
red mullet with vanilla Jerusalem artichoke purée and roasted stem broccoli 92-93
red wine
  gravy 189
  octopus, sweet and sour onions and beef carpaccio 46-48
rhubarb
  poached, rhubarb sorbet and sweet toasted seeds with lemon verbena panna cotta 144-146
  sorbet 198
rice
  chunky mulligatawny 21
  coconut, with roasted spiced lamb 117
risotto, coconut, with lobster pistachio kebabs 72
rosemary oil 193
rosewater and mango sorbet 201

s

salad
  crab, with lemon mayonnaise, smoked paprika honeycomb and pickled apples 70-71
  of English asparagus and scallop, with cockle tartare and mint oil 85
  onion, with baked Cheddar custard 54
  parsley, and red lentil stew, with braised elbow of (shoulder shanks) lamb 118-119
  pea 55-56
  pea, and pea custard, with chicken thighs 100-101
  raw fennel, with rabbit, foie gras and chorizo terrine 58-59
  of shrimps, with watercress, potatoes cooked in butter and poached egg yolk 32
  winter cabbage, with posh sausage roll 33
salmon, curry cured, charred and pickled cucumber and cucumber sorbet 62-63
salsify chips, egg and blue steak 107
sauces
  butterscotch 128-130
  charcuterie 112-113
  cheese 49-51
  chilli 74-75
  fish 189
  GP 52-53
  parsley and wild garlic 108-109
sausage roll, posh, with winter cabbage salad 33
scallop and English asparagus, salad of, with cockle tartare and mint oil 85
sea bass, pan-fried 'heaven and earth', with caviar cream 76-77
seeds, sweet toasted, poached rhubarb and rhubarb sorbet with lemon verbena panna cotta 144-146
service with a smile 73
shortbread, lemon 150
shrimp(s)
  apple and capers with roast pork belly 114-115
  salad of, with potatoes cooked in butter, watercress and poached egg yolk 32
  spiced potted, with coriander and cucumber 73
six-inch string trick 138
sorbet 198-201
  apple 201
  cucumber 62-63
  mango and rosewater 201
  pineapple 201
  rhubarb 144-146, 198
  strawberry 198
  tomato 38-39
soup
  'Birmingham Soup' 1793 18-20
  chunky mulligatawny 21
  easy peasy 22-23
  leek and potato, with crème fraîche, crispy barley and chive oil 24-25
  watercress and wasabi pea 14-15
spaghetti, crispy 49-51
squid, crispy pork-covered, with chilli sauce 74-75
steak, blue, with egg and salsify chips 107

stem broccoli, roasted, and vanilla Jerusalem artichoke purée with red mullet 92-93
stew, red lentil, and parsley salad with braised elbow of lamb (shoulder shanks) 118-119
stock syrup 198
stocks 188
strawberry
  leather 203
  marinated, tarragon and black pepper honeycomb with burnt English custard egg surprise 126, 165-167
  sorbet 198
sweet and sour
  onions, beef carpaccio and red wine octopus 46-48
  parsnips, juniper berries and curly kale with roast loin of venison 120-121
sweetcorn fritters 104-105
syrup
  orange 164
  stock 198
Szechuan pepper
  and almond poached peaches 60-61
  truffled feta, butternut squash and orange terrine 16-17

t

tamarillo and basil jam with lemon and lime posset 140-141

tamarind jam, with duck, liquorice purée and green beans 106
tarragon, black pepper honeycomb and marinated strawberries with burnt English custard egg surprise 126, 165-167
tarts, Bakewell, with double cream ice cream and instant fruit jam 131-133
terrine
  butternut squash, orange, Szechuan pepper and truffled feta 16-17
  rabbit, foie gras and chorizo, with raw fennel salad 58-59
toffee and cumin carrots with brill 84
tomato
  confit cherry tomatoes 194
  tartare, basil oil and tomato sorbet 38-39
trifle, rabbit, pea and black olive, with rabbit lollipops 55-56
truffle, white chocolate and crème fraîche with orange syrup 164
tuile, chocolate 152-153
turbot with scorched lettuce, fondue of onion and crème fraîche 86-87

v

vanilla
  and blackberry baked cheesecake 139
  double cream ice cream 131-133
  ice cream 202
  Jerusalem artichoke purée, roasted stem broccoli and red mullet 92-93

veal, minced belly, Purnell's white pudding 27
vegetables, escabeche of, with beetroot mousse 44-45
venison, roast loin of, with sweet and sour parsnips, juniper berries and curly kale 120-121
vinaigrette 190
vinegar, malt, and black pepper glaze 122-123

w

waffles 182-183
wasabi pea and watercress soup 14-15
watercress
  poached egg yolk and butter, potato cooked in, with salad of shrimps 32
  and wasabi pea soup 14-15
white chocolate
  and coconut ganache 156-157
  and crème fraîche truffle with orange syrup 164
white loaf, simple 172
white pudding, Purnell's 26, 27
wild garlic and parsley sauce 108-109

z

zest, candied 202
zhoug 'my way', confit lemon, and pan-fried roasted cod 91

Acknowledgements

Laura Edwards, for her amazing photography. 'When the curtains are open the shoot is on.'
Rosie Reynolds, for her hard work, great humour and fantastic ideas on the shoots. I loved her look of excitement as she rummaged through my bag!
Polly Webb-Wilson. Brilliant, with great vision, she created a wonderful mood to the book, from driftwood to manhole covers - genius!
Judith Hannam did a brilliant job editing and pulling everything together in such a calm and cool way. Up the Gunners!
My agent and friend **Martine Carter** for making it happen. Legend.
Angela O'Carroll, my PA, sister-in-law and all-round-brilliant Glynn Purnell looker-afterer, for her help throughout the book, particularly the decoding of my handwriting and typing.
Lucy Gowans, for a great layout, and designing and creating a perfect flow throughout.
A special thank you to **Kyle**, for taking a chance and believing in me, and for giving me the opportunity to write.

Kitchen Acknowledgements

For their help with the shoots at the restaurant:
David Taylor, **Luke Butcher**, **Leon Thompson**, **Phil Steggall**, **Kieren Gill**, **Richard West**, **Poppy O'Toole-Downing**, **Thomas Croxford**, **Sam Luckett**. And special thanks to **Private Pile**, aka **Thomas Law**.

This paperback edition published in Great Britain in 2017 by Kyle Books, an imprint of Kyle Cathie Ltd
192-198 Vauxhall Bridge Road, London, SW1V 1DX
general.enquiries@kylebooks.com
www.kylebooks.co.uk

10 9 8 7 6 5 4 3 2 1

ISBN 978 0 85783 424 9

First published as hardback in 2014

Text © 2014 Glynn Purnell
Design © 2014 Kyle Books
Photographs © 2014 Laura Edwards

Glynn Purnell is hereby identified as the author of this work in accordance with Section 77 of the Copyright, Designs and Patents Act 1988.

Editor: Judith Hannam
Editorial Assistants: Tara O'Sullivan, Claire Rogers
Copy Editor: Jo Richardson
Designer: Lucy Gowans
Photographer: Laura Edwards
Food Stylist: Rosie Reynolds
Prop Stylist: Polly Webb-Wilson
Production: Nic Jones, Gemma John

A Cataloguing in Publication record for this title is available from the British Library.

Colour reproduction by ALTA London
Printed and bound in Slovenia byDZS Grafik d.o.o